THE BABES
OF CHRISTMAS

THE BABES OF CHRISTMAS:
CELEBRATING CHRISTMAS WITH GOD'S LOVE FOR PREBORN CHILDREN

Timothy L. Fan

Published by
God-centered Universe Press
Aurora, Colorado
www.gcupress.com

ISBN-13: 978-0-9981369-2-9

All Scripture quotations, unless otherwise indicated, are taken from the World English Bible® (WEB), a modern, public domain translation based on the American Standard Version 1901 Bible, Biblia Hebraica Stuttgartensia Old Testament, and Byzantine Majority Text New Testament. However, the (WEB) Scripture quotations have been adapted in the following manner: (i) the use of the divine name, Yahweh, has been quoted in its traditional English rendering, "the LORD"; (ii) contracted English words have been expanded into their formal equivalents (e.g. "don't" is quoted as "do not"); and (iii) pronouns representing God have been capitalized (e.g. "him," when referring to God, is quoted as "Him").

Scripture quotations marked (KJV) are taken from the King James Version of the Bible.

Scripture quotations marked (NKJV) are taken from the New King James Version®. Copyright © 1982 by Thomas Nelson. Used by permission. All rights reserved.

Cover Original Artwork: "When Baby Jesus Was Born" © I.J. Fan 2016

"But the angel said to him, 'Do not be afraid, Zacharias, because your request has been heard, and your wife, Elizabeth, will bear you a son, and you shall call his name John. You will have joy and gladness; and many will rejoice at his birth. For he will be great in the sight of the Lord, and he will drink no wine nor strong drink. He will be filled with the Holy Spirit, even from his mother's womb. He will turn many of the children of Israel to the Lord, their God. He will go before Him in the spirit and power of Elijah, "to turn the hearts of the fathers to the children," and the disobedient to the wisdom of the just; to prepare a people prepared for the Lord.' " (Luke 1:13-17, WEB)

CONTENTS

TO MY FATHER

Who spent many sleepless nights in the Pediatric Intensive Care Unit caring for God's little ones; who was the "Best Man" at my wedding; and who exhorted me to love the wisdom books of Holy Writ, with a deep, father's love.

AND TO MY CHILDREN

Who have taught me more about the meaning of Christmas than my formal schooling ever could; who already know the sufferings of Christ enough to be Heavenly-minded; and who are loved by their Daddy "all the way to the cross."

PREFACE

Dear Reader,

Christmas should be both joyful and fearful. The love of God, oftentimes meditated upon at length by the true Christian during the Christmas season, is inexhaustibly joyful. At the same time, the awe of the transcendent nature of God, revealed through the earth-shaking voices of the Christmas angels announcing to the shepherds the glad tidings, should cause us to tremble. God is to be feared. The Christ of Christmas is to be feared. Therefore, our Christmas joy should be a trembling joy.

Moreover, to apply the great, timeless doctrines of Christmas to the current horror of the Abortion Holocaust is a fearful task. It is, to be sure, a task that must be done, lest we be found neglecting our King's commandments to *"rescue those who are being led away to death"* (Proverbs 24:11), and to *"love [our] neighbor[s] as [ourselves]"* (Romans 13:9). However, we must tremble at this task. For, who comes to this task with completely clean hands and a completely pure heart? Who is completely free from pride in the midst of his work of Abortion Abolitionism? Who is sufficient for these things?

Let us, then, pray for the all-sufficient grace of God as we plead with Him to guide us in a holy manner in this pursuit of a deeper knowledge of His love for preborn children:

> "O Sovereign Lord, You are our wisdom. The fear of You is our only fount of wisdom. We pray, then, that You would cause our hearts to tremble, with all proper fear and humility, at Your holy Word. Blessed Father, holy is Your name. Teach us to lift up holy hands in prayer as we pray for Your Kingdom to come, on earth as in Heaven, regarding the love that You have for children in the womb. Let Your Holy Spirit open our eyes to see wonderful things in Your Law, and, we pray, glorify Your Son, Jesus Christ, in our hearts as we read. Yours is all dominion and power, all blessing and honor, forever and ever. Amen."

In Christ's Covenantal Love,

Timothy L. Fan
Aurora, Colorado
June 1, 2018

"A relation to Christ will magnify those that are little in the world."

- Matthew Henry

INTRODUCTION:
Relating Christmas to the Plight of the Preborn

WHEREVER the Christmas story is truthfully recounted, the Babe in the manger is at the center of attention. There are, of course, to be mentions of angels, of shepherds, of wise men, and of Joseph and Mary. Yet the Bible puts the Babe at the center of attention, for He is the center of world history. All of world history orbits the little One, the tiny Person who grew and matured in the virgin's womb.

This present, little volume is presented to the Church on account of the conviction that a Christ-centered celebration of Christmas is woefully corrupt without a Christ-centered understanding of God's love for all of the preborn children of the world. That is, to turn a blind eye to the global Abortion Holocaust during the Christmas season, and all in the name of needing to maintain the cozy "positivity" of the season, is not only to betray our preborn neighbors during a critical time of the year; it is also to corrupt our understanding of Christmas itself.

We start, then, by remembering that the incarnation of the Word of God really began nine months prior to the first Christmas. The wonder of the Word becoming flesh and "tabernacling" among us (John 1:14) starts not with the Babe in the manger, but rather with the Babe who was conceived of the Holy Spirit as a single-celled Babe, with full (divine!) Personhood inside of the virgin's womb.[1] Then, as the Babe grew day after day and night after night, He, already being a true, living Human, developed a heartbeat, along with tiny eyes and ears, tiny hands and feet, and a small, tiny little mouth. In a very short time, He kicked in the virgin's womb.

We also start by remembering that the true, historical events surrounding the first Christmas were filled with

---

[1] That is, most likely, her fallopian tube.

iii

danger. Caesar Augustus' tyrannical decree that all peoples under Rome's dominion must go to their ancestral homes to register was probably made without much imperial concern for the multitudinous peasants of the Empire, such as Joseph and Mary, who would have to face many practical hardships as a result of the decree. In the ancient world, it must have been downright dangerous for both mother and Child to travel from Nazareth to Bethlehem in a state of full-term pregnancy.

Yet the greatest danger that happened within two years of the first Christmas was dreadfully dark and terribly atrocious. Under the influence of the spiritual dragon—Satan himself—King Herod, having been outwitted by the wise men, became enraged and ordered that every male child in Bethlehem and in all of its districts, two years of age and under, should be put to death. Thus just as the ancient Hebrew women once wailed beside the Nile River, as their baby boys were so diabolically executed under Pharaoh's murderous decree, so too did the women of Bethlehem weep for their children, with fierce weeping, and refuse to be comforted. At Christmas time, therefore, we must bring to remembrance the dark and dangerous ways in which Satan hates and attacks the children of God, and especially the littlest of His image bearers. At Christmas time, Satan hates all talk of childbearing, for he recalls that at the first Christmas a Child was born, and a Son was given.

Much is at stake here. The lives of millions of children are on the line here. Simultaneously, the historic-Christian understanding of Christmas is at stake here. We cannot celebrate Christmas in a God-pleasing manner without a correct belief in the truths presented herein. Therefore, the present author places this book on the Heavenly altar of God's Heavenly sanctuary, as a pain-soaked labor of love and as a spiritual sacrifice, for the good of His Church and for the remembrance and honor of His littlest martyrs.

Part One:

The Prophetic Babes

THE BABES OF CHRISTMAS

1

THE VIRGIN'S BABE:
The Virgin Birth and Preborn Children

(Isaiah 7:1-25)

In the days of Ahaz the son of Jotham, the son of Uzziah, king of Judah, Rezin the king of Syria, and Pekah the son of Remaliah, king of Israel, went up to Jerusalem to war against it, but could not prevail against it. David's house was told, "Syria is allied with Ephraim." His heart trembled, and the heart of his people, as the trees of the forest tremble with the wind. Then the LORD said to Isaiah, "Go out now to meet Ahaz, you, and Shearjashub your son, at the end of the conduit of the upper pool, on the highway of the fuller's field. Tell him, 'Be careful, and keep calm. Do not be afraid, neither let your heart be faint because of these two tails of smoking torches, for the fierce anger of Rezin and Syria, and of the son of Remaliah. Because Syria, Ephraim, and the son of Remaliah have plotted evil against you, saying, "Let us go up against Judah, and tear it apart, and let us divide it among ourselves, and set up a king within it, even the son of Tabeel."'" (Isaiah 7:1–6)

GOD trembles before no one. He who said, *"Let there be light"* — and immediately there was light — has no fears. He who shook Mount Sinai with the roaring wind of His voice does not quiver before any created thing. Neither storm, nor beast, nor violent army, nor any demonic power in the heavenly realms can cause God to quake with fear. The darkness is as light to Him. As bright as the present is to Him, so too is the future. Therefore, God, the God of Abraham, Isaac, and Jacob, is never afraid.

Christmas, however, calls us, as human beings, to tremble with holy fear. Its roots of tradition are much deeper

3

than the familiar European pastiche of warm gingerbreads, cozy hearths, silky ice skate tracks, and candle-lit evergreen trees. They reach back into the Gospel accounts, themselves. They draw us back into the ancient Scriptures of Israel. Summoning us out of the endlessly subjective routines of personal ambition and acquisition, the roots of Christmas speak to us of God's miraculous invasion into human affairs, and thus of events in history that are both independent of ourselves, and also binding upon our very souls. Our response to these historical events, whether one that moves us towards faith in God or one that drives us deeper into rebellion against Him, charts for us an everlasting course.

What we have, then, in the Christmas accounts of Holy Writ, are neither legends nor myths. We have, instead, accurate and truthful — or, as must be said in loving rebuke to today's blithely apostatizing churches, fully "infallible" and "inerrant" — accounts of real, historical events. Ahaz, the son of Jotham, king of Judah, was truly, historically threatened by a coalition of armies between Syria and Ephraim. Likewise, Mary, the impoverished Jewish woman from Nazareth, was truly, historically *a virgin* when she received the news from the angel Gabriel that she was pregnant with the Baby who was to be named Jesus.

We must, then, allow the Scriptures, and not culture, to define Christmas for us. This means we must approach Christmas with something very different from the mystical, intangible sense of awe and wonder with which it is normally approached today. Instead, we must come to Christmas with the particular, definitive Word of God as our guide. Yet such an approach, which is the only truly Christian kind of approach to Christmas, must cause us to *tremble*. For, when we listen to the story of Christmas in the definitive, biblical language of the seventh chapter of Isaiah, we find our depravity (which is the creeping horror of our own sinful nature) exposed in its holy, divine light.

4

BEWARE OF THE WRONG KIND OF TREMBLING

*David's house was told, "Syria is allied with Ephraim." His heart **trembled**, and the heart of his people, as the trees of the forest **tremble** with the wind.* (Isaiah 7:2)

We ought to tremble before Christ at Christmas time. There is, however, both a right kind of trembling, and a wrong kind of trembling. The difference between the two can be demonstrated by contrasting the heart of Isaiah, the Prophet, with the heart of Ahaz, the king. The latter trembles like the deep maroon leaves of a dogwood tree in an autumn gust of wind, and all before the advancing armies of the enemy nations. He trembles before man. The Prophet's heart, by contrast, does not tremble before enemy threats, for it has already learned what it means to tremble before God.

King Ahaz trembles, albeit wrongly, in the seventh chapter of Isaiah. However, in the preceding chapter, the Prophet himself also trembles. Yet the Prophet's trembling is good. Seeing the Lord on the throne of Heaven, with the train of His robe filling the temple, and with the Seraphim calling out, *"Holy! Holy! Holy! is the LORD of Hosts, the whole earth is filled with His glory!"* the Prophet trembles and cries out, *"Woe is me! For I am undone, because I am a man of unclean lips, and I dwell among a people of unclean lips: for my eyes have seen the King, the LORD of Hosts!"* (Isaiah 6:1-3, 5).

Isaiah's throne room vision of God has taught him the nature of a good and proper kind of trembling. For he, the Prophet, has seen into the very throne room of the Most High! The God before whom the Seraphim tremble is also the Lord before whom even the thresholds of the Heavenly Temple shake and tremble:

The foundations of the thresholds shook at the voice of him who called, and the house was filled with smoke. (Isaiah 6:4)

5

Why does the Prophet tremble? He trembles because He has seen the pre-incarnate Christ in all of His divine holiness.[1] This God, this Lord, has eyes that are too pure to behold evil. His hatred of sin is so great that all who enter into His holy presence without the blood of atonement are immediately struck dead by His divine fire (Leviticus 10:2-3; 2 Samuel 6:7; Acts 5:9-11). The holiness of God causes even righteous men to grow faint in His presence (Daniel 10:8). His countenance is brighter than the sun, shining in its fullness (Revelation 1:16). The Lord's majestic holiness prompts the holy angels to cover their eyes before Him, in fear of Him (Isaiah 6:2). When God's holiness is revealed in His Temple, all cry *"Glory!"* (Psalm 29:9). Therefore, the Prophet Isaiah trembles in a right manner.

Yet while the Prophet trembles rightly, it is wicked King Ahaz who trembles wrongly. Ahaz trembles not before the holy God of Israel, but rather before mere mortals:

> *David's house was told, "Syria is allied with Ephraim."* **His heart trembled**, *and the heart of his people,* **as the trees of the forest tremble with the wind**. (Isaiah 7:2)

King Ahaz has the wrong kind of trembling: he trembles not before God, but rather before men. This can be seen from a different angle by contrasting Ahaz with another king of Judah. As king, Ahaz trembles wrongly. However, there will

---

[1] That Isaiah saw Christ, and not simply a vision of God, in the general sense, is proved in at least two ways. First, in Isaiah 6:1, the Prophet says, *"In the year that king Uzziah died,* **I saw the Lord** *sitting on a throne,* **[exalted]** *and* **lifted up**; *and His train filled the temple."* Yet this must be, at least in some way, a vision of Christ, since Isaiah 52:13 says of Christ, *"Behold,* **My Servant** *will deal wisely. He will be* **exalted** *and* **lifted up**, *and will be very high."* Secondly, the Apostle John, in His Gospel, quotes from the sixth chapter of Isaiah, and then comments on the quotation by saying, *"Isaiah said these things* **when he saw His glory** [i.e. Jesus' glory, see John 12:37], *and spoke of Him"* (John 12:41).

come a king of Judah immediately after him, his son, Hezekiah, who will tremble rightly. Whereas Ahaz trembles before men, his son, Hezekiah, will tremble before God.

It is illuminating to see that both King Ahaz and King Hezekiah are greeted by threats of enemy invasion. Ahaz (in or around 735 BC) is threatened by the invasion into Judah of an enemy coalition between Syria and Ephraim (the Syro-Ephraimite coalition being formed as a way of protecting themselves against the looming military power of Assyria). Similarly, Hezekiah, some thirty-four years later (701 BC), is threatened by an invasion—this time the invasion of the military giant of Assyria, itself.

Moreover, both of these kings of Judah receive news of the terrifying threat of invasion while they are standing at *"the upper pool, on the highway of the fuller's field"*:

> Then the LORD said to Isaiah, "Go out now to meet **Ahaz**, you, and Shearjashub your son, **at the end of the conduit of the upper pool, on the highway of the fuller's field.**"
> (Isaiah 7:3)

> The king of Assyria sent Rabshakeh from Lachish to Jerusalem to king **Hezekiah** with a large army. **He stood by the aqueduct from the upper pool in the fuller's field highway.** (Isaiah 36:2)

Both kings are tested at *"the upper pool."* Both of them receive threats of the imminent invasion of Jerusalem. Yet while Ahaz trembles before men—he is a man of pride and unbelief—Hezekiah responds humbly and faithfully to the threat of imminent invasion by trembling before God:

> David's house [that is, **King Ahaz**] was told, "Syria is allied with Ephraim." **His heart trembled**, and the heart of his people, **as the trees of the forest tremble with the wind.** (Isaiah 7:2)

*When **King Hezekiah** heard it, he tore his clothes, covered himself with sackcloth, and **went into the LORD's house**.* (Isaiah 37:1)

Ahaz trembles before men; Isaiah and Hezekiah tremble before God. There is, then, both a good way to tremble and a bad way to tremble. A king or prophet who gets a bad case of knocking knees before the threats of men is a coward. He cannot please God, for he does not have faith in God. However, a king or prophet who spreads out the written letter of the threats of men before the throne of God, with holy, worshipful trembling, is a man of faith who pleases God. King Ahaz is not such a man.

Yet who are we to blame Ahaz? Is it not natural for a man to fear his enemies, especially when they are much more powerful than himself? Rezin, the king of Syria, and Pekah, the son of Remaliah, king of Israel, have formed a fierce plot against him. They intend to use their military coalition to depose Ahaz (that is, by killing him), and then to set up a puppet-king, the *"son of Tabeel"* (Isaiah 7:6) in his place. Once their puppet-king is established, they will be able to draw Judah (forcibly) into the armed coalition against their great arch-enemy, Assyria.

Therefore, we may say that it is quite "natural" for Ahaz to tremble before these great threats of men. The threat to his own life is very great. However, the reason why Ahaz' trembling before men is very wicked is because he is hard-heartedly rejecting the promises of God's deliverance that are being given to him. The threats of man are great, but the promises of God are greater still. Therefore, to reject these grand promises of God's imminent deliverance is a great wickedness, indeed:

Because Syria, Ephraim, and the son of Remaliah have plotted evil against you, saying, "Let us go up against Judah, and tear it apart, and let us divide it among ourselves, and set up a king within it, even the son of Tabeel." This is what the Lord GOD says: **It shall not stand, neither shall it happen.** *For the head of Syria is Damascus, and the head of Damascus is Rezin; and within sixty-five years Ephraim shall be broken in pieces, so that it shall not be a people; and the head of Ephraim is Samaria, and the head of Samaria is Remaliah's son.* (Isaiah 7:5–9a)

The point, of course, is one of unbelief. Ahaz trembles wrongly because he rejects these great promises, on account of his unbelief. The wrong kind of trembling stems from the wrong kind of heart. It is *a heart filled with unbelief* that produces this wrong kind of trembling. Yet Ahaz ought not to fear men. For, Isaiah gives to Ahaz his own word, the Prophet's Word, that he need not tremble before men:

Tell him, "Be careful, and keep calm. **Do not be afraid, neither let your heart be faint** *because of these two tails of smoking torches, for the fierce anger of Rezin and Syria, and of the son of Remaliah." (Isaiah 7:4)*

However, Isaiah has also warned Ahaz that if he refuses to tremble at the Word of God, then his unbelief will prove to be the cause of his own downfall:

If you will not believe, surely you shall not be established. (Isaiah 7:9b)

Christian Abortion Abolitionists[2] receive many threats from the kingdom of men, and especially at Christmas time. They are warned that their message will be unwelcomed in the contemporary Church, as their humble, yet prophetic portrayals of the evils of contraception[3] and abortion are bound to clash with the contemporary Church's Christmas culture of wealth, joviality, and positivity.[4] They are threatened, also, by professing Christians who believe that their bold (and yet is it not also quite loving?) Abolitionism is a means of driving unbelievers further away from God, and of detracting from "the true meaning of Christmas," as these professing Christians would call it. Therefore, in the face of these threats from the established, contemporary Church (and also in the face of all of the threats that many avowed unbelievers may throw at them for proclaiming Abolitionism at Christmas time), they must learn a different kind of trembling. Instead of trembling, as Ahaz did, before the threats of men, Christian Abolitionists must learn, with ever-increasing integrity, how to tremble before God alone.

What, then, is the right kind of trembling? How should the children of God tremble? The right kind of trembling is a Psalm-76 kind of trembling:

---

[2] The present author defines "Christian Abortion Abolitionists" as those who labor, with cross-carrying labors of love, towards the total abolition of abortion in our world on the basis of their *distinctly Christian convictions*. In other words, they are those who see the total abolition of abortion as both their *Christian duty* and their *doxological service*.
[3] For the "evils" of contraception, see Chapter 2 of the present author's book, *Divine Heartbeat: Listening to God's Heartbeat for Preborn Children* (Aurora, CO: God-centered Universe Press, 2014), 25-43, entitled, "God's Great Blessings: Procreation and Preborn Children." See also this present volume's APPENDIX: "Church History and Contraception: What Historic Christianity Has to Say Against Birth Control," 135-37.
[4] The critics of Abolitionism are, in this instance, quite accurate in their prediction of such a clash. However, they miss the glaring fact that the clash, itself, is really a clash over the Gospel. For, the Gospel of Christ is bound to clash with such an idolatrous Christmas culture in the Church.

*Glorious are you [O Zion], and excellent, more than mountains of game. Valiant men lie plundered, they have slept their last sleep. None of the men of war can lift their hands. At Your rebuke, O God of Jacob, both chariot and horse are cast into a deep sleep. **You, even You, are to be feared.** Who can stand in Your sight when You are angry? You pronounced judgment from heaven. **The earth feared**, and was silent, when God arose to judgment, to save all the afflicted ones of the earth. Selah.* (Psalm 76:4–9)

Also, the right kind of trembling requires the right kind of quiet, confident faith in God:

*For thus said the Lord GOD, the Holy One of Israel, "You will be saved in returning and rest. Your strength will be **in quietness** and **in confidence."** You refused....* (Isaiah 30:15)

Thus proper trembling only comes upon those who have eyes of faith. It is a trembling that believes God's promises, and takes them at face value. By faith, the believer trembles at God's Word, and thus is able to see the threats of men as God sees them.

This means that Ahaz, had he had eyes of faith, would have seen the threats of Rezin, the king of Syria, and Pekah, the son of Remaliah, king of Israel, quite differently. Rather than trembling before them, as one might tremble before a raging forest fire, he would have seen them as two smoldering, burned-out campfire logs. Or, instead of shivering before them, as a man might shiver if two hungry lions were leaping towards him, he would have seen them as two wounded pups, retreating from a fight with their tails between their legs. They plot attack, but God has already promised their defeat.

We must, then, guard ourselves from the wrong kind of trembling. We must not tremble as Ahaz did. With eyes of faith, we must tremble before God, and not before men.

However, the temptation to tremble wrongly is not to be laughed off, as if it were an easy fight. For, even the brave Apostle Peter, who once said to Annas and Caiaphas, the very high priests who had crucified Jesus, *"Whether it is right in the sight of God to listen to you rather than to God, judge for yourselves"* (Acts 4:19), also fell into the sin of the wrong kind of trembling. When the Judaizers, the "circumcision group," pressed him towards separation from eating with Gentile believers, he feared them. He trembled before men:

> But when Peter came to Antioch, I resisted him to his face, because he stood condemned. For before some people came from James, he ate with the Gentiles. But when they came, he drew back and separated himself, **fearing those who were of the circumcision**. And the rest of the Jews joined him in his hypocrisy; so that even Barnabas was carried away with their hypocrisy. (Galatians 2:11–13)

When we face the threats of men, do we have the eyes of faith, or do we have the wrong kind of trembling? Do we tremble before mere mortals rather than before the eternal God?

The society around us says, "It's fine if you want to believe in the Bible and in Jesus as your own, personal faith. But don't you dare accuse all other world religions of being 'blasphemous' and 'wicked'! If you do, then we will be forced to…." When the society around us says this to us, shall we tremble before men, or before God?

Christian parents are very much tempted to tremble before the psychology-based models of parenting that are so inculcated upon us by our culture. These psychology-based models threaten, "If you do not allow your child to be enculturated by television, Facebook, sports stadiums, public schools, and age-segregated socialization, then your child will grow up developmentally stunted and distorted, and thus will come to resent and to hate you." We are tempted to cower before such "professional" threats. When they come, shall we see these threats through the eyes of faith, or shall we tremble before men?

Also, no doubt, the world — the increasingly "Babylonian" world around us — wants to scare us into silence concerning its self-proclaimed right to despise and war against the baby in the womb. Pastors who preach against the sin of contraception are threatened with the loss of their livelihoods. Parents who shun contraception are threatened with the prospect of great financial hardship. Protestant theologians who decry in vitro fertilization (IVF), both in its oftentimes murderous results and in its intrinsic violation of God's design for procreation, are living on the edge of termination by their respective institutions. Christian academic physicians who refuse to be silent about the Abortion Holocaust are very much in danger of academic ostracism. And Christian organizations that publicly advocate laws that would abolish both contraception[5] and abortion are constantly under the threat of public ridicule and persecution.

What, then, shall we do? Shall we tremble before these threats of men? Shall we craft pithy rationalizations, such as, "In the name of expediency..." in order to seek to avoid the

---

[5] When a generation arises in America for whom the very idea of *the abolition of contraception* is a shocking one, we know that we have fallen far away from the Protestant-Christian integrity of Anthony Comstock (1844-1915), who helped craft important United States federal and state laws that prohibited private access to contraception in America for nearly a century (1873-1965 for married couples, and 1873-1972 for unmarried couples). In 1915, Comstock said, "The [legalized] prevention of conception *would work the greatest demoralization,*" and has not this prophetic statement proved frighteningly true in post-1972 America? (qtd. in Mary Alden Hopkins, "Birth Control and Public Morals: An Interview with Anthony Comstock," *Harper's Weekly* [May 22, 1915], Michigan State University scanned copy, n.p. [cited January 19, 2015]. Online: http://www.expo98.msu.edu/people/comstock.htm, emphasis added).

real sufferings that our convictions may bring upon us? Or shall we tremble before God, and not before men?

Much is at stake here. Certainly, the lives of little ones, residing in their mothers' wombs, are at stake. Yet it may be truly said that *even our ability to understand Holy Scripture is at stake here*. For, if we tremble wrongly, then we will, inevitably, read the Scriptures wrongly.

BEWARE OF THE WRONG KIND OF SCRIPTURE READING

Immediately, however, someone will object: "But this means that you are accusing not a few pastors of having the wrong kind of trembling. You are saying that they tremble before men, rather than before God. And yet these pastors preach the Bible. They say that they believe the Bible, in its entirety, and they quote verses from the Bible in plenty, just as you do. They simply do not interpret the Bible according to your own narrow, judgmental Abolitionist schemes."

In response, it must be said that there is a vast difference between *claiming* to interpret Scripture rightly and *actually* interpreting Scripture rightly. For, is it not true that *the wrong kind of trembling* will inevitably produce *the wrong kind of Scripture reading*?

Ahaz trembles wrongly. As a result, Ahaz, who *claims* to interpret Scripture rightly, *actually* interprets the Bible wrongly. He twists and distorts the Scriptures:

> *The LORD spoke again to Ahaz, saying, "**Ask a sign** of the LORD your God; ask it either in the depth, or in the height above."*
>
> *But Ahaz said, "**I will not ask, neither will I [test] the LORD**."* (Isaiah 7:10–12)

Ahaz is no simpleton. He knows the Bible. However, since he trembles wrongly—before men and not before

God—he also interprets Scripture wrongly. He dares to challenge the Prophet to a Bible duel. Instead of trembling, joyfully, before the Prophet's Word of promise and assurance, he instead rejects that Word by thrusting Holy Scripture at it. Yet he thrusts wrongly. He twists the Law of Moses in his cowardly efforts to evade the Prophet's Word:

> But Ahaz said, "I will not ask, **neither will I [test] the LORD.**" (Isaiah 7:12)

Ahaz is, no doubt, quoting from the sixth chapter of Deuteronomy:

> **You shall not [test] the LORD your God,** as you [tested] Him in Massah. (Deuteronomy 6:16)

Yet Ahaz is not to be commended for this. His rejection of the "sign" from the Lord (Isaiah 7:11) is not admirable. He is not piously evading a trap set for him by a false prophet, using Holy Scripture for his source of discernment. Rather, he is perverting the Scriptures in order to avoid having his own unbelieving heart exposed by the Prophet. For, the true meaning of the commandment not to "test" the Lord is that it is a grave warning against *unbelief*:

> Therefore the people quarreled with Moses, and said, "Give us water to drink" [which is a statement of unbelief].

> Moses said to them, "Why do you quarrel with me? **Why do you test the LORD?**" (Exodus 17:2)

However, like all false teachers of the Bible, Ahaz is subtle and crafty. He knows the story of Gideon, wherein Gideon "tested" the Lord by demanding first a wet fleece, and then a dry fleece, all in order to shore up his own doubts (Judges 6:36-40). Ahaz thus applies a "never ask a sign from the Lord—no exceptions" rule to the Word of the Prophet Isaiah. With a touch of pious pretense, then, he throws Deuteronomy 6:16 right in the face of the Prophet: "*You shall not [test] the* LORD *your God.*"

The brazen pride of Ahaz is astonishing. His willingness to interpret Scripture wrongly, all in order to avoid the Prophetic exposure of his own sinful trembling before men, is both glaring and shameful. Had he lived after the time of Jesus, he might even have been so wicked as to quote the Lord Jesus in defense of his sinful unbelief, falsely claiming that Jesus would not permit him to ask Isaiah for a *"sign"*:

> *But [Jesus] answered them, "**An evil and adulterous generation seeks after a sign**, but no sign will be given it but the sign of Jonah the prophet."* (Matthew 12:39)

Who, then, is right, and who is wrong? Is the Prophet Isaiah wrong to tell Ahaz to ask for a sign from the Lord? Or is Ahaz wrong in his daring interpretations of the Scriptures? Is it *always* testing God when one asks Him for a sign? Apparently, God Himself does not think so:

> *He said, "Listen now, house of David. Is it not enough for you to try the patience of men, **that you will try the patience of my God also**?"* (Isaiah 7:13)

The irony is that Ahaz has missed the whole point about what the Bible says concerning *"testing"* God:

> *He called the name of the place Massah* [meaning, "Testing"], *and Meribah* [meaning, "Contention"], *because the children of Israel [contended], and because they **tested** the* LORD, *saying, "**Is the** LORD **among us, or not?**"* (Exodus 17:7)

"Testing" God, then, is a matter of unbelief. It is not asking the Lord for a sign, per se, that constitutes the sin.

Rather, *"testing"* God is a posture of unbelief towards Him. For, the heart of the Israelites who demanded of the Lord water in the wilderness is exposed by their question, *"Is the LORD among us, or not?"* (Exodus 17:7). They are *"testing"* the Lord by refusing, hard-heartedly, to believe His promises. Ironically, this is exactly what King Ahaz is doing in front of the Prophet Isaiah!

There are, in fact, faithful and righteous ways to ask God for miraculous signs in the Bible. Moses, for example, asks God for help in knowing how to win the favor of his fellow Israelites. God responds by giving Moses three miraculous *"signs"* (Exodus 4:8-9). Also, Jesus Himself does not seem to mind it when His disciples ask Him for a *"sign"* concerning *"the end of the age"*:

> As he sat on the Mount of Olives, the disciples came to Him privately, saying, *"Tell us, when will these things be? **What is the sign** of your coming, and of the end of the age?"* (Matthew 24:3)

Instead of accusing them of *"testing"* Him, Jesus actually gives them a *"sign"* to look for:

> *...and then **the sign** of the Son of Man will appear in the sky. Then all the tribes of the earth will mourn, and they will see the Son of Man coming on the clouds of the sky with power and great glory.* (Matthew 24:30)

The point, then, is that Ahaz' rejection of the sign of God is a matter of the wrong kind of trembling — trembling before men — which produces the wrong kind of Bible reading. In turn, we know that this wrong kind of Bible reading — the unbelieving kind — is serious business because God chooses to discipline it severely. Ahaz, who has sinfully trembled before the Syro-Ephraimite coalition, which was, itself, designed to ward off Assyria, shall now have to face the wrath of Assyria, who will turn the pleasant vineyard of Judah into a land of *"briers"* and *"thorns"*:

> *It will happen in that day that the* LORD *will whistle for the fly that is in the uttermost part of the rivers of Egypt, and for the bee that is in the land of Assyria. They shall come, and shall all rest in the desolate valleys, in the clefts of the rocks, on all thorn hedges, and on all pastures. In that day the Lord will shave with a razor that is hired in the parts beyond the River, even with the king of Assyria, the head and the hair of the feet; and it shall also consume the beard. It shall happen in that day that a man shall keep alive a young cow, and two sheep; and it shall happen, that because of the abundance of milk which they shall give he shall eat [curds]: for everyone will eat [curds] and honey that is left within the land. It will happen in that day that every place where there were a thousand vines at a thousand silver shekels, shall be for* **briers and thorns**. *People will go there with arrows and with bow, because all the land will be* **briers and thorns**. *All the hills that were cultivated with the hoe, you shall not come there for fear of* **briers and thorns**; *but it shall be for the sending out of oxen, and for the treading of sheep.*
> (Isaiah 7:18–25)

The wrong kind of trembling produces the wrong kind of Scripture reading. Those who tremble before the threats of men, rather than trembling before God, shall inevitably interpret the Holy Scriptures wrongly. Their sinful hearts blind them to the proper meaning of the Bible. Then, due to their self-exalting, man-fearing approach to Scripture, they shall have to face severe chastisement from the Lord.

Three times Isaiah prophesies about *"briers and thorns"* that shall overtake Judah as a result of Ahaz' twisted Scripture reading—a twisted reading that led him to reject the Prophet's Word. These *"briers and thorns"* harken back to the fifth chapter of Isaiah, wherein God promises to judge Judah, His wicked and wayward *"vineyard"* by turning it into a place of *"briers and thorns"* (Isaiah 5:3-6). Now, due to King Ahaz' wrong kind of Scripture reading, resulting from his rejection of God's supernatural sign of salvation to him, this judgment will fall upon Judah.

The wrong kind of trembling produces the wrong kind of Scripture reading, and the wrong kind of Scripture reading can be extremely dangerous for the Church. Thus a professing-Christian pastor, when he trembles before men rather than before God, preaches his way through the Gospel of Matthew, verse by verse, by trumpeting "grace" to the point of distorting it, altogether, while at the same time blunting all of Matthew's sharp edges on the eternal truths of the doctrine of Hell. He makes room in his study of the Sermon on the Mount for "Christian homosexual identity," and he employs the verse, *"Do not judge, so that you will not be judged"* (Matthew 7:1) for the purpose of denouncing and shaming a Christian man in his church, whom he dubs a "legalist Christian," because that man dares to assert, with tears of love, that unrepentant fornicators and homosexuals, even if they claim to have "prayed the prayer of salvation," cannot inherit the Kingdom of God.

Again, bad trembling produces bad Bible reading. How, then, does the Bible speak to the Church concerning the scientific theory that the earth is "billions of years old"? Also, what do the Holy Scriptures truly say about Darwin's theory of evolution? What does God's Word actually say about the innovative theory of animal carnivorism existing before the Fall of Adam? How does the Word of Christ speak to the novel interpretative theory that Noah's Flood was localized, rather than global? How many of the "new interpretations" of the first eleven chapters of Genesis may be rightly exposed as heresies — being rooted in trembling before men, rather than trembling before God alone?

Moreover, why should there be any major disagreement at all concerning what God's Holy Word has to say to the abhorrent concept of "family planning" (natural or

19

otherwise)? Also, should we not be greatly ashamed of the fact that professing Christians actually argue over "whether or not the Bible is silent on the personhood of the newly conceived baby in the womb"? Moreover, concerning those children who have been born, safely, into professing Christian homes, why should there be any major debate, whatsoever, over the question of what the Bible has to say concerning the proper content of a Christian child's course of education?[6] Are not the very presence of these debates symptomatic of a very large number of professing Christians who tremble before men, rather than before God?

Therefore, take heart, beloved Brother or Sister, you who have labored in love to win your neighbor to the right kind of Scripture reading, but seemingly to no avail. The Prophet Isaiah understands your pain. Or, better put, you have been invited to obtain a small share *in his pain*. Like him — yet his words are the very Words of inspired Scripture, while your words are merely a recounting of the already-inspired Scripture — you have faithfully delivered the Word of God to your neighbor. Like the Prophet Isaiah — yet your sufferings admittedly have been less pure and less costly than his — you have discharged your evangelistic duty with love, and with tears. Therefore, the pain that you feel in your being despised and rejected by men, even by your own family members or friends, is a share in the Prophet's pain. Thus you who have had a share in the Prophet's pain may also

----

[6] Healthy debate there may be in the particular nuances of the content of a Christian child's course of education, but the idea of any debate at all concerning the major thrusts of the content (i.e. "biblically saturated in all disciplines" versus "humanistic/secular — fallaciously cast in a 'neutral' mold") ought to be anathema, in light of historic Christianity. Also, the present author sees no other primary model of education in Scripture than that of parent-child, Word-centered education (and, therefore, Christian home education ought to be the primary model of education for Christians). For this, see Deuteronomy 6:6-9; 11:18-21; Proverbs 1:8-9; 4:1-4; 6:20-23; Psalm 78:5-6; 2 Timothy 1:5; etc.

now look forward, according to the promise of our Lord Jesus Christ, to the Prophet's reward (Matthew 5:12).

THE RIGHT KIND OF SCRIPTURE READING

If King Ahaz' example is a wicked one, warning us that the wrong kind of trembling produces the wrong kind of Scripture reading, then the Prophet Isaiah, himself, is a godly example, set before us for our instruction. He, the Prophet, trembles rightly before the holy, holy, holy God of Israel. Therefore, he, the Prophet, is the only one in this account who can interpret the *"sign"* correctly.

> Ask *a sign* of the LORD your God; ask it either in the depth, or in the height above. (Isaiah 7:11)

Here, then, is the *right* interpretation of the *"sign"* given by the Lord. It is Isaiah, and not Ahaz, who has the right kind of interpretation of the *"sign"*:

> Therefore **the Lord Himself will give you a sign**. Behold, **the virgin will conceive, and bear a son, and shall call his name Immanuel**. He shall eat [curds] and honey when he knows to refuse the evil, and choose the good. For before the child knows to refuse the evil, and choose the good, the land whose two kings you abhor shall be forsaken. (Isaiah 7:14–16)

The right kind of Scripture reading includes a virgin and her son, named Immanuel. The name Immanuel means, "God with us." This is, then, no ordinary child. Yet who is the *"virgin"* in verse 14? The question is difficult, and it calls for a very careful kind of Scripture reading, the kind that trembles at God's Word.

The Hebrew word for *"virgin"* is *b^ethûláh (pronounced: beh-thoo-la)*. However, what makes the question of the identity of the *"virgin"* in verse 14 difficult is that here, in verse 14, we do not have the Hebrew word *b^ethûlâh*, which would mean *"virgin"* in straight-forward fashion. Rather, what we actually have in verse 14 is the Hebrew word *'almáh (pronounced: al-**ma**)*, which means "a young maiden (either married or unmarried)." Therefore, questions immediately arise. Is she really a virgin? Is she married? Who is she? And who is her son?

There is some mystery here, since this *"maiden"* is somehow to be identified with—but only partially identified with—the wife of the prophet Isaiah. For, Isaiah 7:14 says that *"the [maiden] will **conceive, and bear a son**…"* and, not long after this prediction, Isaiah 8:3 mentions Isaiah's wife as one who both *"conceived"* and *"bore a son"*:

> *I went to **the prophetess**, and **she conceived**, and **bore a son**. Then the LORD said to me, "Call his name 'Maher Shalal Hash Baz.'"* (Isaiah 8:3)

This, in turn, fulfills the prophecy of chapter 7, the one that wicked King Ahaz refused to believe:

> *He shall eat [curds] and honey when he knows to refuse the evil, and choose the good. For **before the child knows** to refuse the evil, and choose the good, the land whose two kings you abhor [the land of Damascus and Samaria] shall be forsaken.* (Isaiah 7:15–16)

> *I went to the prophetess, and she conceived, and bore a son. Then the LORD said to me, "Call his name 'Maher Shalal Hash Baz.' For **before the child knows** how to say, 'My father,' and, 'My mother,' the riches of **Damascus** and the plunder of **Samaria** will be carried away by the king of Assyria."* (Isaiah 8:3–4)

Thus Maher Shalal Hash Baz is the son of the maiden. He fulfills the prophecy, *but only partially*.[7] And this is the mystery of the virgin birth. For, according to the ninth chapter of Isaiah, the *"sign"* of the *"the son"* that is given in Isaiah 7:14 cannot be fully fulfilled in Maher Shalal Hash Baz. This is because Maher Shalal Hash Baz, the prophetess' son, fails to fulfill both the *royal* and the *divine* credentials of *"the son"* of whom the ninth chapter prophesies:

> *For to us **a Child** is born. To us **a Son** is given; and the government will be on his shoulders. His name will be called Wonderful Counselor, Mighty God, Everlasting Father, Prince of Peace.* (Isaiah 9:6)

What, then, is the right kind of Scripture reading regarding this *"sign"* from God? The right kind of interpretation of the *"sign"* involves a double-fulfillment. First, it refers, in general, to *Isaiah's own son*. For, the Prophet's children are, no doubt, *"signs"* from God:

> *Then the LORD said to Isaiah, "Go out now to meet Ahaz, you, and Shearjashub* [meaning: 'A Remnant Will Return'] ***your son**, at the end of the conduit of the upper pool, on the highway of the fuller's field."* (Isaiah 7:3)

Again,

> *I went to the prophetess, and she conceived, and bore **a son**. Then the LORD said to me, "Call his name Maher Shalal Hash Baz* [meaning: 'Swift to the Spoil, Quick to the Plunder']*."* (Isaiah 8:3)

---

[7] Note that the Septuagint, the ancient Greek translation of the Hebrew Old Testament, uses *parthénos*, the Greek word for *"virgin,"* to translate the Hebrew *'almáh*. This adds to the mystery of Isaiah 7:14 — a mystery that is only revealed in the New Testament Gospels.

And again,

> *Behold,* **I and the children** *whom the* LORD *has given me* **are**
> **for signs** *and for wonders in Israel from the* LORD *of Hosts,*
> *who dwells in Mount Zion.* (Isaiah 8:18)

Children are signs from God. Isaiah's children have names that connote both judgment and salvation, all at once. Thus in order to announce the Gospel of His *only-begotten Son*, God does not use a strong warrior, clad in armor. Nor does He employ a brilliant scribe, clad in doctoral robes. Rather, God chooses a weak, fragile, dependent *child* as His sign of ultimate judgment and ultimate salvation.

Why, then, are even professing Christian people warring against children through contraception and abortion? Are children not, each and all, miraculous "signs" to us of God's love for the world, revealed in the Gospel? The Prophet Isaiah says that none of them—not even a single one of these precious "signs" from God—should ever be considered burdensome, unnecessary, or unwanted.

Think upon the baby in the womb. Consider his unique fingerprints, specially carved by God nine to ten weeks after conception. Observe, in your mind, the delicate, fragile little fingers, pulsating with life—yet easier to overlook than alpine forget-me-nots—that are tipped by those fearful and wonderful prints. Consider, also, his heartbeat, only three weeks after conception, more vivacious than the strong tide of the sea, racing with life. Who, then, has the right to murder, in the womb, even a single one of these miraculous "signs" from God?[8] And if our society thinks that, by way of medical hook or political crook, it has the societal right to murder these precious "signs" of the Gospel that God has granted to us in the womb, is not our society calling down

---

[8] The Gospel calls for the total abolition of abortion, without exceptions.

upon its own head the furious judgment of the Lord of the Heavenly Hosts?

Think also upon a godly Christian home, filled and overflowing with godly offspring (see Psalm 127:3-5 and Malachi 2:15). If the Lord blesses that home with a multitude of children,[9] consider carefully the preciousness of each child. Each one of the seven, ten, fourteen, or even nineteen placemats at the family dinner table represents a child who is a "sign" of hope and salvation from the Lord. Each one of the many occupied pillows in the home, in the quiet of night, is happy to have its occupant. For, which one of these precious "signs" from God should have been prevented through contraception? What "greater good," coming at the expense of one of these precious little lives, could these parents have effected through the use of birth control? Are not relatively empty houses and relatively empty church worship services (relatively empty of children, that is) very severe judgments from God?

But alas! Isaiah's wife, the prophetess, cannot completely fulfill the *"sign"* of Isaiah 7:14. For, the ninth chapter of Isaiah ties the *"sign"* to *a divine Son:*

> *For to us **a Child** is born. To us **a Son** is given; and the government will be on his shoulders. His name will be called Wonderful Counselor, **Mighty God**, Everlasting Father, Prince of Peace.* (Isaiah 9:6)

---

[9] In Scripture, a multitude of children is a blessing from the Lord, but the converse is not true. Barrenness and bereavement are not necessarily signs of the Lord's curse. Instead, many times God grants the heavy crosses of barrenness and bereavement to His most prized and godly servants. Note the following instances of this: Genesis 18:10; 25:21; 29:31; Exodus 1:21; 2:9; Judges 13:2; Ruth 4:16-17; 1 Samuel 1:10 (and following); 2 Samuel 12:24-25; 1 Kings 17:23; 2 Kings 2:21; 4:16-17; Esther 2:7; Job 1:18-19; Psalm 113:9; Isaiah 7:14; 49:20-21; 54:1; Jeremiah 31:15-17; Hosea 1:8-10; Luke 1:5-7; 7:12-14; and Hebrews 11:11.

The complete fulfillment of Isaiah's prophecy will have to wait for another Child who is *"a sign,"* or, better put, *"the Sign"* from God. That Child appears in the New Testament book of Revelation:

> *A great* **sign** *was seen in heaven: a woman clothed with the sun, and the moon under her feet, and on her head a crown of twelve stars.* **She was with child. She cried out in pain, laboring to give birth.** *Another sign was seen in heaven. Behold, a great red dragon, having seven heads and ten horns, and on his heads seven crowns. His tail drew one third of the stars of the sky, and threw them to the earth. The dragon stood before the woman who was about to give birth, so that when she gave birth he might devour her Child.* **She gave birth to a Son, a male Child**, *who is to rule all the nations with a rod of iron. Her Child was caught up to God, and to His throne.* (Revelation 12:1–5)

The wrong kind of trembling produces the wrong kind of Scripture reading. However, the right kind of trembling, which leads to the right kind of Scripture reading, always points us to this *"Sign"* from God: *Christ, Himself.* When we tremble before the infinite holiness of God in the sixth chapter of Isaiah, then we learn how to read the seventh and eighth chapters of Isaiah rightly. We find in the prophecy of Isaiah 7:14 the doctrine of the virgin birth. The Babe of Isaiah's prophecy is, in the prophecy's ultimate fulfillment, the eternal Son of God, dwelling in real, human flesh.

This, then, calls for joyful trembling! The Gospel contained within Isaiah 7:14 is *joyful*, since the Son of the virgin is named *"Immanuel,"* which means, *"God with us!"* The fullness of deity dwells bodily in the fragile frame of this baby Boy. God visits man in the flesh of a joyfully kicking, joyfully burping Babe. We see the Babe, and hear His name, and realize that in Him we have God residing among us!

*Therefore the Lord Himself will give you a sign. Behold, the virgin will conceive, and bear a son, and shall call his name **Immanuel**.* (Isaiah 7:14)

However, the Gospel contained in the name *"Immanuel"* is not only joyful. It is also fearful. We must *tremble* at the sound of Immanuel's name, for His name is a sign both of joyful salvation and of dreadful judgment:

*Inasmuch as these people refused the waters of Shiloah that flow softly, and rejoice in Rezin and in Remaliah's son; now therefore, behold, the Lord brings up over them the waters of the River, strong and mighty — the king of Assyria and all his glory; he will go up over all his channels and go over all his banks. He will pass through Judah, he will overflow and pass over, he will reach up to the neck; and the stretching out of his wings will fill the breadth of Your land, **O Immanuel**!* (Isaiah 8:6-8)

Immanuel saves. Immanuel also judges in wrath. Therefore, Christmas is joyous. Yet Christmas is also fearful. For, at Christmas time we treasure the Babe who came to demonstrate the infinite love of God contained within such a tiny, swaddled bundle. At the same time, we remember that that precious bundle of joy in Mary's arms is also the eternal God, whose throne the Prophet saw, and before whom the Prophet felt undone! Immanuel's love is infinitely stronger than that of a nursing mother for her own nursing infant (even as she caresses and memorizes the delicate shapes of her baby's hands), and yet Immanuel's wrath is also infinitely fiercer than that of a bear robbed of her cubs. The Holy One of Israel has taken on babyhood. Yet the Babe of Isaiah 7:14 also has infinite holiness and power, such that the earth trembles at His presence and the mountains melt like wax before Him. Mortal eyes, filled with wonder and amazement, look down upon and behold the Babe, but the holy angels of Heaven cover their eyes in fear of Him as they worship Him.

What a wondrous "Sign," then, of the biblical meaning of Christmas! In order to celebrate Christmas, we must come to Him, the little God-infant wrapped in swaddling clothes. Therefore, if we have the right kind of Scripture reading, we shall feel compelled by the Gospel *to bow down and worship this Babe.* We shall confess that He is both divine and human, both Man and God.[10] All babes of Christmas are breathtaking "signs" from God, but all babes, save Christ alone, are mere finite creatures. It is this Christ Babe, and no other, whom we worship, with great fear and joy, at Christmas.

This is the right way to read Isaiah's prophecy concerning the virgin's Son. It is the way of worship. We interpret *the Sign of God* to be *the Son of God.* And once we see, through repentant eyes of faith, the Son of God wrapped in a body ever so small and fragile, lying in a manger, we fall down upon our faces and worship this divine Babe of Christmas, with much fear and trembling. Amen.

---

[10] At the Incarnation, the eternal Son of God took on a human nature. His essence did not change. Rather, He retained all of His divine attributes. At the same time, He did assume a *full* human nature. Therefore, Jesus Christ is one, eternal Person, now existing in two distinct natures, without confusion or mixture of the natures. This is in line with the historic formulation of the Creed of Chalcedon (AD 451).

2

THE ROYAL BABE:
The Messiah's Government and Preborn Children

(Isaiah 9:1-7)

But there shall be no more gloom for her who was in anguish. In the former time, He brought into contempt the land of Zebulun and the land of Naphtali; but in the latter time He has made it glorious, by the way of the sea, beyond the Jordan, Galilee of the nations. The people who walked in darkness have seen a great light. Those who lived in the land of the shadow of death, on them the light has shined. (Isaiah 9:1–2)

GOD, in His infinite wisdom, uses the created order for the purpose of teaching us how, properly, to understand contrasts. For the sake of our instruction, the Creator has built many meaningful contrasts into His meticulously-crafted creation. It is God, for example, who intentionally places tiny, unobtrusive wildflowers near the summits of enormous, craggy mountains. He does this in order to teach us the contrast between our own, tiny, human finitude, and His own, enormous, divine infinitude. Thus His creative contrast, between alpine flowers and alpine summits, is our necessary lesson in the "doctrine of God."

Think, then, upon the vast riches of wisdom and knowledge that our Creator has built into His creation through contrasts. God has made the piercing joy of new life — a whole new person packaged in a tiny baby's body — to exist in sharp contrast to the painful sword of personal bereavement. He has made some things hot, and others cold (and, according to Revelation 3:16, He does not care much for churches that are lukewarm). The Lord has made certain objects razor-sharp, such as the eagle's talons, and other objects delicately soft, such as the fur of the Holland Lop. In the study of the solar system, we know that God has caused the earth to tilt on its axis, such that the poles of the earth experience, yearly, both polar days and polar nights. The polar days, on which the sun never sets, are quite the contrast to the polar nights, on which the sun never rises.[1]

All of these contrasts that God has built into the created order have important things to teach us about the Christian truths of Holy Scripture. The wise individual will meditate upon them and immediately begin to see their implications for understanding God's holy Word.

Moreover, history itself is replete with important contrasts that are told and retold for our instruction. For example, the study of church history tells us that some of the greatest doctrines of the faith are best learned by contrasting them with their corresponding heresies. That is to say, it is much harder to learn the doctrine of the Trinity (that God is one in essence, but three in Persons) by itself, than it is to learn about it while contrasting it with the ancient heresies of wicked men the likes of Sabellius and Arius (both of whom denied the Trinity, though in quite different ways).

Or, as it is no easy thing to learn the doctrine of Christ (which describes the one Person, the Son of God, now existing in two distinct natures, one fully divine and the other fully human), even when contrasting it with the ancient heresies of men such as Apollinarius and Eutyches (both of whom grossly distorted the doctrine of Christ, but each in a different manner), it is certainly much more difficult to study the doctrine of Christ without these ancient

---

[1] Not a few of these contrasts result from Adam's original sin. That is, the "threatening" nature of many of them is a warning that tells us of the consequences of sin, and of our need for repentance towards God. For example, neither the scorching hotness of fire, nor the icy coldness of snow were life-threatening realities prior to Adam's sin. The contrasts of creation, therefore, are, in many instances, signs of the Fall of Adam.

contrasts. Heresy, once exposed as heresy, only serves to clarify sound doctrine. Or, to put it the other way around, the truths of Christianity are seen with a much greater lucidity once they are shown to exist in great contrast to all error and falsehood.[2]

What, then, of the glaring contrast that exists, today, between God's love for little babies, and our society's hatred towards them? If babies are so prized by their Creator, why are they now being murdered (via abortion), prevented (via contraception), experimented upon (via human embryonic stem cell research), frozen (via in vitro fertilization), and discarded (via abandonment) in such heart-rending numbers? Does not God's gargantuan love for babies exist in sharp contrast to the Western world's attitude towards them? And does not this explain why we, in the West, are ever so quickly losing our love for Christmas? Does not this have a lot to do with the now culturally-enforced linguistic changes from "Merry Christmas" to "Seasons Greetings," and from "Christmas trees" to "Holiday trees"? Is not the Christ of Christmas the *Babe* of Christmas? And, therefore, does not our disdain for a vast multitude of babies (a disdain which arises in the name of a false god called Population Control, among other names) in the West betray one of the underlying reasons for our rejection of the true Christianity of Christmas?

---

[2] This is not to suggest that sin is essential for understanding holiness (via contrast), nor that falsehood is essential for understanding truth (via contrast). May it never be! For, if that were the case, then God's holiness and faithfulness could never be enjoyed, in perfect love, apart from the experiential knowledge of good and evil. Yet we know that God neither willed nor desired Adam and Eve to obtain such experiential knowledge. Rather, He abhorred their willful decision to do so. As the Apostle Paul so somberly puts it, *"Why not (as we are slanderously reported, and as some affirm that we say), 'Let us do evil, that good may come?' Those who say so are justly condemned"* (Romans 3:8).

Christmas is not only about a miraculous Babe (Isaiah 7:14); it is also about *a royal Babe.* The Christmas account takes us to the birth of the great, high King. The Baby who is born is, in fact, the King of kings. This is the greatest birth of all time, for it is the most royal birth of all time. It announces God's offer of peace to the world. It also proclaims the inauguration of God's Kingdom in the world. Yet in order to witness, through the lens of the ninth chapter of Isaiah, this splendid, royal birth, we must first learn to see the great contrasts built into this majestically-composed chapter. There are three such contrasts, the first of which involves the sharp contrast between darkness, with its gloomy cloud, and light, with its bright sun.

THE GREAT CONTRAST BETWEEN DARKNESS AND LIGHT

The first poetic contrast in Isaiah 9:1-7 is one between darkness and light:

> *They will pass through it, very distressed and hungry; and it will happen that when they are hungry, they will worry, and curse by their king and by their God. They will turn their faces upward, and look to the earth, and see distress, **darkness**, and the **gloom** of anguish. They will be driven into **thick darkness**.*

> *But there shall be **no more gloom** for her who was in anguish. In the former time, He brought into contempt the land of Zebulun and the land of Naphtali; but in the latter time He has made it glorious, by the way of the sea, beyond the Jordan, Galilee of the nations.*

> *The people who walked **in darkness** have seen **a great light**. Those who lived in the land of **the shadow of death**, on them **the light** has shined. You have multiplied the nation. You have*

increased their joy. They rejoice before You according to the joy in harvest, as men rejoice when they divide the plunder. (Isaiah 8:22–9:3)

The end of the eighth chapter and the beginning of the ninth chapter of Isaiah are both shrouded in darkness. There is a thick, ominous fog looming over the land of Israel, and it is a very dark fog. Much like the plague of thick darkness that God brought upon Pharaoh, king of Egypt, Israel's thick darkness is a judgment for her thick, dark sin against God. The darkness is so dense that one can barely see his own hand in front of his face, much less the path in front of him.

Darkness, then, is a judgment for Israel's sin. In particular, this *"shadow of death"* (Isaiah 9:2) kind of darkness that Israel is experiencing can certainly be described as a judgment from God:

*Give glory to the LORD your God, before He causes **darkness**, and before your feet stumble on **the dark mountains**, and, while you look for **light**, He turns it into **the shadow of death**, and makes it **gross darkness**.* (Jeremiah 13:16)

However, not all darkness is of the judgment kind. Sometimes in the Bible this kind of "Death-shadow darkness" describes suffering for righteousness' sake:

*All this has come on us, yet have we not forgotten You, neither have we been false to Your covenant. Our heart has not turned back, neither have our steps strayed from Your path, though You have crushed us in the haunt of jackals, and **covered us with the shadow of death**.* (Psalm 44:17-19)

Psalm 23 certainly describes a kind of "Death-shadow darkness" which falls upon the innocent: that of persecution for the sake of righteousness. Though David is hunted by his enemies (Psalm 23:5), and though he must *"walk in the valley of the Death-shadow,"* he says, *"I will not fear evil, for You are with me"* (v. 4).[3] Therefore, not all who experience the gloomy cloud of "Death-shadow darkness" are under the judgment of God.

We can surmise, then, that at the opening of the ninth chapter of Isaiah, there are two kinds of people living in Israel. There are wicked idolaters, who profess to know God but by their deeds prove otherwise. They are judged by the Lord with this Death-shadow cloud hanging over their heads. At the same time, however, there are pious Israelites who are enduring the moral darkness of their age, suffering alongside of their countrymen, yet in their case, only for the sake of righteousness. In both situations, the people are desperate for light. The former are desperate for God's light of grace and forgiveness, which comes, ever so mercifully, to those who will repent and believe in Him. The latter are desperate for God's liberating light, coming to illuminate the dark prison cells of their prolonged persecutions and other righteous sufferings.

Gloriously, then, this deep darkness, dreadfully called the "Death-shadow darkness," exists in poetic contrast to a great light that comes from God. The darkness is thick and horrible, but there is a bright, gleaming light that is found bursting into the history of Israel:

> *The people who walked in **darkness** have seen **a great light**. Those who lived in the land of **the shadow of death**, on them **the light has shined**.* (Isaiah 9:2)

The contrast is blindingly bright! The Death-shadow is a form of deep darkness, but the light from God is now piercing, and gleaming:

---

[3] The present author's translation.

*For You will **light my lamp**, O LORD. My God will **light up my darkness**.* (Psalm 18:28)

The distinct contrast is between the deep darkness of the Death-shadow that has fallen upon Israel and the gleaming light of God that shall come to Israel. This is glad tidings! The darkness of human sin, and of all of the suffering caused by it, shall be pierced through by the sharp arrow of God's divine light!

Yet the most glorious thing about this impending visitation of light into such a darkened world is that the brightness of the light comes from a supernatural source. This is not a man-made, technological solution to the problem of darkness. Rather, the source of the light that is about to come to Israel is God, Himself:

*At the **brightness** before **Him** His thick clouds passed, hailstones and coals of fire.* (Psalm 18:12)

The Prophet Ezekiel once saw a vision of a dark, ominous storm cloud coming upon Israel from the north (Ezekiel 1:4). Yet in the middle of this dark cloud, he saw bright, blinding flashes of light. At first, he considered the fearsome angels, the four living creatures whom he saw in the midst of the storm cloud, to be the source of the brilliance of the light. However, once he saw that the four living creatures were the guardians of a great throne, he realized that the source of the blinding light—which was as threatening as a raging fire and, simultaneously, as beautiful as golden beryl or sunlit amber—was the One who was seated upon that throne. Having seen the appearance of the likeness of the glory of the Lord, Ezekiel fell facedown before Him.

For Death-shadow-enshrouded Israel, there is a light that is about to dawn. Its source is not one of nature, nor of man. Rather, its source is God, Himself!

His splendor is like the sunrise. Rays shine from His hand, *where His power is hidden.* (Habakkuk 3:4)

This is wonderfully mysterious. The great contrast between darkness and light in the ninth chapter of Isaiah intends to do more than give us a few gleams of hope in the midst of gloomy times. It actually intends, in some mysterious way, to reveal God to us!

The people who walk in darkness shall see a great light. This light is a gleaming light that comes from God, Himself. For *"**God is light**, and **in Him is no darkness at all**"* (1 John 1:5). He, the light of the world, is coming. He, Immanuel, shall come to be the light of God, and thus "God with us." And so let darkness-drenched Israel say, "The light of God shall come to rescue us, and the darkness shall not defeat Him."

Of course, once the meaning of this stark contrast between darkness and light is revealed — that God Himself is coming to save Israel — then joy inevitably follows:

*You have multiplied the nation. You have **increased their joy**. They **rejoice** before You according to the **joy** in harvest, as men **rejoice** when they divide the plunder.* (Isaiah 9:3)

There is four-fold rejoicing in verse 3, and this *"rejoicing"* over God's coming *"light"* culminates in the book of Isaiah with a vision of Heaven, itself:

*Arise, shine; for **your light has come**, and the LORD's glory has risen on you. For, behold, **darkness will cover the earth**, and **thick darkness** the peoples; but **the LORD will arise on you**, and His glory shall be seen on you. Nations will come **to your light**, and kings to **the brightness of your rising**.* (Isaiah 60:1–3)

Therefore, God's Heavenly *"light"* produces a Heavenly *"rejoicing"*:

> But be glad and **rejoice** forever in that which I create; for, behold, I create Jerusalem to be **a [rejoicing]**, and her people a joy. I will **rejoice** in Jerusalem, and delight in My people; and the voice of weeping and the voice of crying will be heard in her no more. (Isaiah 65:18–19)

A prisoner of war, who has been fighting on the side of his righteous king, suffers in prison for his righteous cause. Unwilling to join other prisoners in being "eagerly reeducated" in the murderous ideologies of the kingdom of Darkness, against which his king's army fights, he finds himself in solitary confinement, in an underground prison cell that lets no light, at all, come into the cell. All is dark, almost pitch black, in his torturous condition.

Yet one day, after years of living in this awful darkness, the prison guard, whom he has secretly won over to friendship, brings his usual, meager breakfast to him, dull flashlight in hand, along with a secret message of great hope. The guard whispers to him, excitedly, "Your king is winning the war against our people. His troops are approaching our capital city, even sometime this month!"

Then, only a few weeks later, the languishing prisoner of war sees something that he has not seen in years. He sees a bright, beaming light! It is spilling under his prison cell door and into his cell. The light signals his liberation! Even before the heroic rescue soldiers — sent by his king, who has triumphed — burst across the remaining feet of the underground corridor that leads to his cell, and even before they throw open the door, setting him free from his torturous confinement, he rejoices! Seeing the brightness of the king's soldiers' searchlights, a brightness that is piercing through the crack beneath his prison door, is enough to cause him to rejoice with great tears of rejoicing!

The Apostle John speaks of such a glorious, liberating light:

*In the beginning was the Word, and the Word was with God, and the Word was God. The same was in the beginning with God. All things were made through Him. Without Him was not anything made that has been made. In Him was life, and the life was **the light of men. The light shines in the darkness, and the darkness has not overcome it**.* (John 1:1–5)

Jesus Christ *is* that gleaming light sent from God. *He* dispels the darkness of human sin and the Death-shadow of the kingdom of Satan. *He* is the light that has dawned upon those living in darkness. On the cross, His light was snuffed out for the punishment of our own sins—He did not swoon, but actually *died* on the cross. Yet on the third day, the stone covering His tomb was rolled away, and the light of His victorious resurrection burst into the tomb, conquering the darkness!

What, then? Shall unbelievers continue to hate the light? Fearing the exposure of their sinful habits and wicked deeds, shall they go on refusing to enter into the light of Christ? Shall they continually refuse to let their sins be revealed in the light, in order that those sins might be repented of, forgiven, and cleansed away? As children of darkness, are they still unwilling, even now that the true Light of the world has come, to forsake the darkness, to be born of the Holy Spirit, and to learn to walk in the light, as children of light? If they are so continually unwilling, then God is proved just and merciful, even as their wicked ingratitude for His sacrifice on their behalf has earned them a severe condemnation:

*They will turn their faces upward, and look to the earth, and see distress, **darkness**, and the **gloom of anguish**. They will be driven into thick darkness.* (Isaiah 8:21b-22)

For true believers, however, God, who said, *"Let light shine out of darkness,"* has made the light of Christ shine in our hearts. The new creation, marked by His light, has been wrought within us. Therefore, since His light lives in us, we are *"the light of the world"* (Matthew 5:14).

The question, then, is whether or not we ourselves are willing to shine our light brightly before men. At present, the world around us is falling into a deep, wicked darkness. That is, the once Gospel-bright light of American society has now come to hate the light of Jesus with an intensity of hatred that is unprecedented in the history of our nation. Sometimes, then, knowing how much the world around us hates the gleaming light of Christ, we, as Christians, become afraid and begin to hide our light. We begin to dim the light within us so that we are not so easily recognized by the world, and subsequently persecuted by the world.

However, the call of Jesus is that we always, without fear of men, allow our light to *gleam* before a watching world. There is, then, both a warning and an assurance issued to the American Church of today. The warning is that if we do not shine our light brightly in America, then the light of the Gospel will soon be snuffed out in America, just as it is being snuffed out so rapidly in much of Western Europe. The assurance, on the other hand, is that if we do let our lights gleam, in brightness, through the American Church, God shall be with us. We may, indeed, face much persecution. Yet the darkness will not overcome us.

These, then, are pivotal times for Christians in the Western world. We have a history-changing decision to make. Namely, will we shine our light brightly into the darkening world around us? Or will we hide it? The future of our own offspring hangs upon this decision. Moreover, in a multitude of ways, the future of Western Civilization hangs upon the decision of the Western Church (that is, what remains of the Western Church), at this very hour.

THE GREAT CONTRAST BETWEEN WAR AND PEACE

There is a second poetic contrast in Isaiah 9:1-7. This is the great contrast between war and peace. Israel has seen the brutality of war. Her Messiah, however, will be a Prince of Peace:

> *For the yoke of his burden, and the staff of his shoulder, the rod of his oppressor, you have broken as in the day of Midian. For all the armor of the armed man in the noisy battle, and the garments rolled in blood, will be for burning, fuel for the fire. For to us a Child is born. To us a Son is given; and the government will be on His shoulders. His name will be called Wonderful Counselor, Mighty God, Everlasting Father, Prince of Peace. Of the increase of His government and of peace there shall be no end.* (Isaiah 9:4–7a)

War, human war, is a horrible result of the curse of sin. Contra pacifism, let it be said that in a sinful world war is, sometimes, a necessary event, even for the righteous.[4] Yet war, in general, is a brutal affair. The victims of oppressive war campaigns, in specific, never delight in war.

Throughout her history, Israel has been brutalized by not a few oppressive, warring nations. The brutality of this is symbolized, in verse 4, by the tyrannical *"yoke"* of Midian:

> *For **the yoke** of his burden, and the staff of his shoulder, the rod of his oppressor, you have broken as in the day of Midian.*

---

[4] In this regard, it is worth noting that Balthasar Hubmaier, the greatest of the Anabaptist theologians, and also a humble martyr, had the courage to oppose Luther's "bondage of the will," on the one hand, and yet to stand against the Swiss Anabaptists in their pacifist views regarding the sword, on the other hand. See his *On the Sword*, in *Bathasar Hubmaier: Theologian of Anabaptism* (trans. H. Wayne Pipkin and John H. Yoder; Scottdale, PA: Herald Press, 1989), 492-523.

Early on in her history, Israel wore the *"yoke"* of Egypt. This is the back-breaking, murderous *"yoke"* that the Lord, on her behalf, broke off during the Exodus out of Egypt:

I am the LORD your God, who brought you out of the land of Egypt, that you should not be their slaves. **I have broken the bars of your yoke**, *and made you go upright.*
(Leviticus 26:13)

However, in the Law, God warns Israel that if she rebels against Him, she shall wear the *"yoke"* of war and oppression, again:

Because you did not serve the LORD your God with joyfulness, and with gladness of heart, by reason of the abundance of all things; therefore you will serve your enemies whom the LORD sends against you, in hunger, in thirst, in nakedness, and in lack of all things. **He will put an iron yoke on your neck**, *until He has destroyed you.* (Deuteronomy 28:47–48)

Perhaps the most vivid picture of this war-filled *"yoke"* of oppression is found in the sixth chapter of the book of Judges. It is here that the horrible *"yoke"* of *"the hand of Midian,"* to which the Prophet Isaiah refers, is made terribly manifest:

The children of Israel did that which was evil in the LORD's sight: and the LORD delivered them into **the hand of Midian** *seven years.* **The hand of Midian** *prevailed against Israel; and* **because of Midian** *the children of Israel made themselves the dens which are in the mountains, and the caves, and the strongholds. So it was, when Israel had sown, that the* **Midianites**, *the Amalekites, and the children of the east came up against them. They encamped against them, and destroyed the increase of the earth, until you come to Gaza. They left no sustenance in Israel, and no sheep, ox, or donkey. For they came*

41

up with their livestock and their tents. They came in as locusts for multitude. Both they and their camels were without number; and they came into the land to destroy it. **Israel was brought very low because of Midian;** *and the children of Israel cried to the LORD.* (Judges 6:1–6)

Israel has been terrorized by war, by the *"yoke"* of her enemies. Midian, then, is simply symbolic of the heaviest kind of this war-forced *"yoke"* that Israel must carry upon her back. And in Isaiah 9:4, this yoke is exceedingly heavy, pressing hard and sharp into her *"shoulder"*:

For the yoke of his burden, and the staff **of his shoulder,** *the rod of his oppressor, you have broken as in the day of Midian.*

Like a cross on her back, the brutalities of war and slavery have been borne by Israel on her *"shoulders."* This is the *"yoke"* that God shall break. This is the cross that He Himself shall lift from her *"shoulders."*

In distinct contrast, then, to these great oppressions of war, which are epitomized by the evil oppressions of Midian, the government of the coming Messiah shall bring peace to Israel. For, instead of putting an oppressive burden on the *"shoulders"* of His conquered subjects, this coming King will carry the heavy weight of the government *on His own "shoulders"*:

For all the armor of the armed man in the noisy battle, and the garments rolled in blood, will be for burning, fuel for the fire. For to us a Child is born. To us a Son is given; **and the government will be on His shoulders.** *His name will be called Wonderful Counselor, Mighty God, Everlasting Father,* **Prince of Peace.** *Of the increase* **of His government and of peace** *there shall be no end….* (Isaiah 9:6–7a)

In Isaiah's prophecy, then, there is an enormous contrast between war and peace. The *"armor of the armed man"* and the *"garments rolled in blood"* in verse 5 stand in great contrast to the *"Prince of Peace"* at the end of verse 6. Former kings have oppressed Israel with unthinkable brutality. But this new King, the Prince of Peace, will rule Israel with complete justice and uncompromising righteousness. The wars of Israel's oppression will cease, and the peace of her Messiah will reign.

Yet how so? How does the Messianic King bring this peace? God has certainly promised it:

> *"I create the fruit of the lips: **Peace, peace,** to him who is far off and to him who is near," says the* LORD, *"and I will heal them."* (Isaiah 57:19)

Again, however, we ask, "How shall this be accomplished? In a sinful world full of such brutal and bloodthirsty peoples, how can God ever bring this kind of perfect peace? What shall cause wars to cease for all of the righteous?" The answer to these questions is, actually, a violent one. It is the violence of the cross—human violence perpetrated against the sinless, spotless Lamb of God—that, through the riches of the mercy of God, brings about peace for all true believers:

> *But He was **pierced** for our transgressions. He was **crushed** for our iniquities. The punishment that brought **our peace** was on Him; and by His wounds we are healed.* (Isaiah 53:5)

Jesus Christ could have come to Jerusalem, during His First Advent, on a war horse. He had every right to let His wrath blaze hot and unquenchable against all of sinful humanity. He could have drawn His sword, being supported by legions of His holy angels, and brought the full slaughter of wicked humanity to completion. However, had He executed justice that way—and it would have been more than just!—none would have been saved. All would have been lost. From Adam to the generation present at His First Advent (which, then, would have been His only advent), all would have perished, everlastingly, in Hell.

Instead, in His great, covenantal love, He came to wicked humanity in a posture of divine humility. In His compassion towards rebellious sinners, He chose to enter Jerusalem on a peaceful animal. He rode into Jerusalem on a donkey:

> *Rejoice greatly, daughter of Zion! Shout, daughter of Jerusalem! Behold, your King comes to you! He is righteous, and having salvation;* **lowly, and riding on a donkey**, *even on a colt, the foal of a donkey.* **I will cut off the chariot from Ephraim, and the horse from Jerusalem; and the battle bow will be cut off;** *and* **He will speak peace to the nations**: *and His dominion will be from sea to sea, and from the River to the ends of the earth.* (Zechariah 9:9–10)

Abraham brought Isaac to God's altar, being willing, by faith, to sacrifice his only son to God, in obedience to God's command. Abraham brought Isaac to God *on a donkey* (Genesis 22:3, 5). Yet while God provided a ram as a substitute sacrifice in Isaac's stead, there was no such provision for His only-begotten Son. Jesus rode *a donkey* into Jerusalem, and, subsequently, the Father in Heaven looked away as the knife was lowered upon His beloved Son. On the cross, Jesus was fully human, dying a substitutionary death for the sins of humanity. Yet on the cross, He was also fully God, which means that His blood was valuable enough to pay for the sins of the whole world.[5]

Jesus has brought *peace* to us, who believe, by winning *the war* against Satan, sin and death. This was a war that He fought His whole earthly life, but He won the war at the great Battle of Calvary. There, with blood dripping down His face and His body shivering with pain, *Jesus brought peace to us by dying on the battlefield for us.* There, at the cross, He won the war. The Prince of Peace conquered on the battlefield of the cross. For Christians, then, the terrors of war have ceased, and the peace of God has come to reign in our hearts.

However, we do great violence to this precious prophecy in the ninth chapter of Isaiah if we assume that the mighty contrast between war and peace found in the Gospel means that our lives, as Christians, ought to be filled with serenity. Now is not the time of situational serenity for Christians. Consider, for example, the life of the blessed Apostle Paul. Did he understand the great contrast between war and peace in the ninth chapter of Isaiah? Certainly, he did. Was his life one of cozy comforts and situational serenity? Certainly, it was not. He lived and died as a martyr on the battlefield of the Gospel. And yet, through all of his sufferings, Paul could still say that he had found a *"peace"* that *"surpasses all understanding"* (Philippians 4:7).

Thus the Christian life is not situationally serene, but there is, nevertheless, a definitive contrast between war and

---

[5] The atonement of Christ is *universal in potential*, since the blood of Jesus is valuable enough to pay for the sins of all men, everywhere, despite the severity of the worst sins of the worst of sinners (1 John 2:2). However, the atonement of Christ is certainly *very limited in application*, which means: (i) it is only applied to the elect, to those who receive Him by believing in His name; and (ii) those multitudes of unregenerate professors of Christianity who dangerously presume upon the atoning blood of Christ actually trample it underfoot—to their own condemnation in the everlasting burnings of Hell (Hebrews 10:29).

peace built into it since, for Christians, the *war with God* has ceased. As Christians, we know that we were conceived and born as enemies of God. We grew up fighting against God, and, consequently, God's justice and wrath fought against us. Yet when we were converted, born of the Holy Spirit, our war with God ceased. The blood of Jesus was the peace offering that paid the justice penalty (the death penalty) for our treasonous rebellion against God, and thus reconciled us to God. In Christ, we have peace with God. We, who used to be rebels, are now called children of the Most High.

Do you feel that God is at war with you? It may be that you are not yet a Christian. You can, in fact, be a baptized, reliable church attender and still not be a genuinely Spirit-reborn Christian. Perhaps you feel that God is at war with you because you have been "faking it" your whole life. Your lips have professed to know God, but your deeds have proved otherwise. You have not been born again. Your mind is controlled by the thinking of your sinful flesh. Your thoughts are at enmity with God. Thus His wrath is kindled against you, even as you read this book.

If so, beloved Sinner, *now is the time to repent.* If you do not repent and turn to God, through the blood of Christ Jesus, His war against you, due to your sins against Him, will continue forever, in Hell. Yet if you will but turn to God in repentance, with a tearing of your heart over the grievous nature of your sins against Him, and if you will but cast your soul upon Him, in faith, crying out for Jesus Christ to be your sole Lord and God, then you can know the peace of God. He will put His Holy Spirit in you, make you a new creation in Christ Jesus, and you will know His peace and favor that He extends to those who are truly His own, who truly belong to Him.

Again, do you feel that God is at war with you? If you are a genuine Christian, if you know that the Holy Spirit resides in you (and one way that you know this is through His placing in you a deep hatred of sin and a deep desire to obey the Law of Christ), then remember that God is no longer at war with you. The sins of your past, no matter how heinous they were, have been blotted out through the blood of the Lamb.

God is not against you, O Christian, but for you. Even when He smites you, He does it because He disciplines the children that He loves. Or, when He allows you to suffer for no specific sin of your own, but righteously and perseveringly, He is allowing you to share in the fellowship of His sufferings. Precious Christian Brother or Sister, God is not at war with you. He loves you. He is fighting *for you*.

How, then, does this Gospel of peace speak to the true "War on Women"[6] that is being waged against women through feminism, pornography, sexual immorality, contraception, and abortion? How can there ever be peace in society when society wages war against its own women and children? How can the men of a given society claim to love truth and justice, when at the same time they turn a blind eye to the ravenous war that is being fought in their own cities and homes against the chastity of women and the sacredness of life in the womb?

---

[6] At the time of this writing, the pro-abortion media is conditioning its readers and viewers into seeing Christian Abolitionism as an evil ideology by labelling it as a "War on Women." By this, the pro-abortion media means that Christian Abolitionist policies against contraception and abortion are an attack on so-called "women's reproductive health" and, in regard to abortion, the supposed "woman's right to choose." This is nothing less than Satanic language (see Genesis 3:4-5). The truth is that feminism, pornography, sexual immorality, contraception, and abortion all wage a brutal war against God's created design for women. They attack womanhood itself. Also, abortion kills *female* preborn children. Therefore, abortion wages war against women from conception all the way through motherhood, and on into advanced stages in life (for example, what measure of twisted sinfulness is required to bring about the living contradiction of a "pro-contraception, pro-abortion *grandmother*"?).

The true "War on Women" is Satan's global-feminist rampage against the very nature of biblical womanhood. In this war, Satan has many ideological misfits enrolled in his army. He also has his four-star generals leading his dark troops (who are deceptively clothed in uniforms of light): General Gender Equality (otherwise known as General Non-Submission of the so-called "Salvation Army," who is a feminine general), General Seductive Immodesty (also a feminine general), General Women's Workforce (who is, ironically, a male general), General Birth Control (the son of the famed five-star general, General Sexual Immorality), General Abortion Rights, and General Women's Rulership (the youngest and most powerful of the three feminine generals). Thus Satan has cunningly enlisted both men *and women* into his army in order to fight a global campaign against the very nature of womanhood.

Yet the Gospel of peace has the power, through the blood of Jesus Christ, to cleanse women from the guilty stains of their proud feminisms, and, under the headship of Jesus Christ, to protect and provide for women who are seeking shelter from the devastations of this feminist war. It restores Christian women to the joy and glory of female submission (1 Corinthians 11:15).[7] It invites them out of the workforce and back into the peaceful harbor of the Christian home (Titus 2:4-5).[8] This Gospel of peace restores the unity of Christian marriage to the lives of women whose

---

[7] The Gospel, in restoring women to the glory and joy of submission, which mirrors the joy and glory of Jesus' submission to the Father, nevertheless does not teach a blind, "door mat" form of submission. For, a Christian woman is accountable first to God, and only then to her father, her husband, or her pastor. Therefore, there are times when biblical "submission" requires a Christian woman to "obey God rather than man" (see, for example, Exodus 1:17; Esther 4:11; 1 Peter 3:2).
[8] The home is one of the most important mission fields in the world, as proved both by biblical history and by church history. Yet it is not without its great sufferings and crosses (Genesis 3:16).

marriages have been divided by the cruel forces of a dual career family, reuniting husband and wife under a single economic mission and family vision. It also restores the unspeakable joys of childbearing[9] to the lives of Christian women. For, once a Christian mother realizes the far surpassing value of motherhood over career-hood, she has been set free from the tyranny of modern feminism. Watching her sons run down a grass-blanketed hill, their heads tilted back with laughter, on a bright, weekday mid-morning, or singing her infant daughter to sleep on a snowy, crisp winter's afternoon, she realizes that the Gospel of peace has put an end to the feminist war within her heart.

However, there is another war, a blood-soaked war, being fought in the realm of the family. It is the war between parents and their own children. Both contraception and abortion have created a great war between parents and their children.[10] Through contraception and abortion, parents indulge the darkest, most diabolical parts of their sinful hearts by learning to despise their own offspring, calling them "unwanted children." Instead of eagerly desiring them, counting them as amongst God's greatest gifts to them (yet still lower, of course, than God's indescribable gift of Himself to them), these parents loathe their own children.

In turn, the children learn to despise their own parents. If, for example, grown children discover that they are merely

---

[9] In the cases of single women, barren wives, or bereaved mothers, the "unspeakable joys of childbearing" are still present in the Gospel of peace, and even magnified by it, through the Heavenly fruitfulness of *spiritual childbearing*.

[10] Space does not permit us to expand on how *institutionalized education* has also created a giant war between parents and their children. Yet it certainly has done so. The "teen culture's" despising of the Fifth Commandment provides some of the strongest evidence of how horrible this war really is. In time, history will show just how much modern, institutionalized "parenting" through modern, institutionalized education has damaged, if not destroyed parent-child loyalty, and thus parent-child discipleship, in the home.

the "select few" who escaped the great Contraceptive Prevention, and also the "survivors" of the great Abortion Holocaust, they will eventually come to understand their relatively small valuation in the eyes of their parents. It is no wonder at all, then, that they will quickly and impassively transfer their loyalty away from their parents and to their ravenous packs of peers, even at young ages. It is also no surprise that when their parents reach their elderly years, these same children will toss them, hurriedly, into nursing homes. They intuitively know that they were not as "wanted" as children as they had hoped to be "wanted," and, therefore, they are quite indifferent about the question of whether or not their parents should feel "wanted" in their own infirmities of old age.

Still, the Gospel of peace can cause this war between parents and children to come to an end. In the Gospel, God turns the hearts of fathers to their sons, and the hearts of sons to their fathers (Malachi 4:6). In the great Gospel of Christ, parents who have aborted their own offspring find the unspeakable freedom of the complete forgiveness of their crimes, and the ineffable hope that one day they will be reunited, in complete peace, with their aborted offspring, in Heaven! It is the blood of Jesus Christ alone that reconciles husband to wife, and parent to child, for that blood alone has the power to reconcile man to God, and man to man.

THE FINAL, APOCALYPTIC CONTRAST

There is one final, poetic contrast in Isaiah 9:1-7. It is a big, apocalyptic one. It is the contrast between the kingdom of Midian, with all of its horrific oppression, and the Kingdom of Christ, with all of its Heavenly glory:

> *For the yoke of his burden, and the staff of his shoulder, the rod of his oppressor, you have broken as in **the day of Midian**.* (Isaiah 9:4)

This "kingdom of Midian" is in apocalyptic contrast to,

*For to us a Child is born. To us a Son is given; and the government will be on His shoulders. His name will be called Wonderful Counselor, Mighty God, Everlasting Father, Prince of Peace. Of the increase of His government and of peace there shall be no end, **on David's throne, and on his kingdom**, to establish it, and to uphold it with justice and with righteousness from that time on, even forever. The zeal of the LORD of Hosts will perform this. (vv. 6-7)*

We have learned, already, of the wickedness of Midian. The monstrous war crimes of the kingdom of Midian have made it an apocalyptic symbol for the kingdom of Satan. At the end of the Bible, in the book of Revelation, this dark, diabolical imagery of the kingdom of Satan reaches its most frightening stature in the apocalyptic kingdom of "Babylon." This "Babylon" will outdo even Midian in wickedness:

*I heard another voice from heaven, saying, "Come out of her, my people, that you have no participation in her sins, and that you do not receive of her plagues, **for her sins have reached to the sky**, and God has remembered her iniquities."*
(Revelation 18:4-5)

In sharp, apocalyptic contrast to the kingdom of Midian (and, ultimately, the kingdom of Babylon), it is the *"Child,"* the *"Son"* of Isaiah's prophecy, who brings the Kingdom of Heaven to earth. At the end of world history, the kingdom of Midian shall fall. Yet the Kingdom of God shall prevail, for that Kingdom shall be carried upon the shoulders of God's Anointed, His Christ. His Kingdom alone shall endure.

Here, then, is the *royal* Babe of Christmas. Here is the *Kingdom* Babe who is scorned and rejected by the world (whose rejection, in turn, explains the world's disdain for children and rejection of Christmas). The *royal* Babe of

Christmas is revealed to us through His *royal titles* in
Isaiah 9:6:

His name will be called **Wonderful Counselor***….*

The term *"Counselor"* in this prophecy is not the kind of
"counselor" whom misguided Westerners see when they
feel depressed.[11] Rather, the word *"Counselor"* refers to a
governing advisor, or a wise governor.[12] Also, the term
"Wonderful" does not mean "artistically or sensorially
inspiring," as most English speakers would take it. Rather, it
refers to the miracle-working nature of God.[13]

Thus when Jesus responds to the challenges of the
Pharisees and scribes with supernatural words of divine
wisdom, He is a *"Wonderful* **Counselor***."* He alone possesses
the perfect, governing wisdom of the Most High. Also, when
He miraculously heals sick people in the streets, He is
fulfilling the title *"****Wonderful*** *Counselor."* For the miracles of
Jesus prove that He is the incarnate God. He alone can work
the *wonders* of God by His own *wondrous* power.

Who is the royal Babe? He is the *"Wonderful Counselor."*
He is also:

*…****Mighty God****….*

---

[11] As the Christian antithesis to the mass worship of modern psychology
in the Western world, should not pastors know both their Bibles and
their people well enough to shepherd their hurting church members
through their sorrows in a distinctly God-fearing, Scriptural manner?
[12] For the Hebrew term *yôʿeṣ* representing a governing advisor, or wise
governor, even as God is the ultimate *"Counselor,"* see:
1 Chronicles 27:32-33; Job 3:14; Psalm 16:7; and Isaiah 40:13-14.
[13] See, for example, the *"wonders"* of God, all connected to the Person and
nature of God, in: Exodus 15:11; Judges 13:18-19; Job 37:14-16;
Psalm 77:11, 14; and 139:14. Also, for God Himself as a *"Wonderful
Counselor,"* see: Job 42:3; Isaiah 25:1 and 28:29.

This means much more than that Jesus Christ is a "powerful" God. It means, literally, that He is the *"Mighty-warrior God."* In 1 Samuel 16:18, David is called a *"mighty warrior."* The same Hebrew term is used here in Isaiah 9:6, *"Mighty-warrior God."* Christ is a *"Mighty-warrior God."* He is the Warrior described in Psalm 45:3: *"Strap Your sword on Your thigh, [O Mighty-warrior]: Your splendor and Your majesty."* This, then, is a divine title. For the *"Mighty-warrior"* is also *"God"*: *"Your throne, O God, is forever and ever. A scepter of equity is the scepter of Your Kingdom"* (Psalm 45:6).

Thus when the book of Revelation says that Jesus, upon His Second Coming, will return as a Warrior, riding on His war horse, we immediately think of Jesus as the *"Mighty-warrior God"*:

> *I saw the heaven opened, and behold, a white horse, and He who sat on it is called Faithful and True. In righteousness **He judges and makes war**.* (Revelation 19:11)

Thus far, then, the royal Babe is both *"Wonderful Counselor"* and *"Mighty God."* Yet He is also, thirdly:

*...**Everlasting Father**....*

This is breathtakingly clear. The Messianic King *must be divine*, for He is called *"Everlasting Father."* This is a title that can only belong to God Himself. God is Israel's Father, and God alone is *"Everlasting Father"*:

> *For You are our **Father**, though Abraham does not know us, and Israel does not acknowledge us. You, O LORD, are our **Father**. Our Redeemer from **everlasting** is Your name.* (Isaiah 63:16)

Who is the royal Babe of the Kingdom of God? He is *"Wonderful Counselor,"* and *"Mighty God,"* and also *"Everlasting Father."* And His fourth and final title is:

...*Prince of Peace*....

Blessed are the peacemakers, yes, but only because they exclaim with their voices, "Blessed is the Prince of Peace!" Through Jesus, we have peace with God: *"Being therefore justified by faith, we have peace with God through our Lord Jesus Christ..."* (Romans 5:1). Also, Jesus' royal reign will bring complete peace on earth: *"Of the increase of His government and of peace there shall be no end..."* (Isaiah 9:7). Sadly, not all will share in this peace. Many will be shut out of this Kingdom of peace, for *"there is no peace...for the wicked"* (Isaiah 48:22). Yet for those who know the royal Babe of Isaiah's prophecy, who love and worship this Babe, there will be peace without end. The Prince of Peace will rule over a Kingdom of Peace, and His peace shall continue forever and ever.

Therefore, when we gaze upon the royal Babe in Isaiah 9:6, the great contrast between the kingdom of Midian and the Kingdom of Christ becomes cosmically sharp. Midian is a kingdom of sin, oppression, and death. Christ's Kingdom is one that is ruled by a Miracle-working Governor, a Mighty-warrior God, and an Everlasting Father, who is also the Prince of Peace.

Abortion, then, is really the battle between two cosmic kingdoms. In the kingdom of Midian, which becomes (in the book of Revelation) the kingdom of "Babylon," there is always a "Pharaoh" who seeks to take all of the little Hebrew babies and murder them in the Nile River. In Babylon's kingdom, there is always a "Herod" who is seeking to slaughter the little ones of Bethlehem. While under the rule of Babylon, Rachel always weeps for her children.

Yet in the Kingdom of Christ, things are not so. In His Kingdom, there are little baby "arks" to save the babies from drowning in the Nile River. In Christ's Kingdom, there are dreams sent from God that rescue little children from the wrathful slaughter of Herod. Under the glorious, peaceful rule of Christ, every little one in the womb, from conception onwards, and especially the ones with the smallest frames, are treasured by God and by all who walk in His light.

In actual human history, the sharp, apocalyptic contrast between the kingdom of Midian and the Kingdom of Christ crystallized, no doubt, when Jesus Christ was born as a Babe in Bethlehem. At that time, the great contrast became one of Caesar Augustus, king of Rome, versus the poor Jewish Babe in the manger. Later on, it became one of the wicked oppression of Rome versus the frailty of the infant Church. Ultimately, as we have said, it becomes the sharp contrast between apocalyptic Babylon and the coming Kingdom of Heaven.

How, then, do you, dear Reader, look upon this royal Babe? When you look upon this Babe in the manger at Christmas time, what do you see? Do you see an archaic religious icon that is too outmoded to matter anymore? Do you see a "Western myth" that promotes "spiritual bigotry" against those who have hoarded wealth in the last days, or against those who, supposedly, have been genetically programmed to be homosexuals?[14] In other words, do you view the Babe of Christmas through the dark, gloomy lens of man-invented ethics and the *religion* of Secular Humanism?

---

[14] In God's eyes, homosexuality is an *"abomination,"* as it is written: *"If a man lies with a male, as with a woman, both of them have committed an abomination: they shall surely be put to death; their blood shall be upon them"* (Leviticus 20:13). It is not a genetically-fixed identity. Rather, it is quite *"against nature"* and contrary to *"the natural function"* (Romans 1:26-27). As such, both unrepentant homosexuals and those who approve of their lusts and sinful actions cannot inherit the Kingdom of God (Romans 1:32; 1 Corinthians 6:9-10).

Or, do you see the truth? Do you see the true light, the divine light, piercing through the darkness of human lies and human sin? Is your formerly darkened heart sufficiently pierced by this light, and your brazenly blackened pride sufficiently slain by this light, such that you can see, by faith, the holiness of this Babe of Bethlehem, and thus tremble, with holy fear, before His blindingly luminous manger? Do you see that this human Babe, in His full humanity, is also the royal Babe, in His full divinity? If so, does not the very sight of this royal Babe summon you to repentance, and call you to live, by faith, a life that is so lit up by the holiness of Christ that it exists in vivid contrast to an ever-darkening world?

Now when Jesus heard that John was delivered up, He withdrew into Galilee. Leaving Nazareth, He came and lived in Capernaum, which is by the sea, in the region of Zebulun and Naphtali, that it might be fulfilled which was spoken through Isaiah the prophet, saying,

"The land of Zebulun and the land of Naphtali, toward the sea, beyond the Jordan, Galilee of the Gentiles, the people who sat in darkness saw a great light, to those who sat in the region and shadow of death, to them light has dawned."

From that time, Jesus began to preach, and to say, **"Repent! For the Kingdom of Heaven is at hand."**
(Matthew 4:12–17)

Amen.

3

THE ANCIENT BABE:
Christ's Eternality and Preborn Children

(Micah 5:1-6)

Now you shall gather yourself in troops, daughter of troops.
He has laid siege against us. They will strike the Judge of Israel
with a rod on the cheek. But you, Bethlehem Ephrathah, being
small among the clans of Judah, out of you One will come out to
Me that is to be Ruler in Israel; whose goings [forth] are from of
old, from [everlasting]. (Micah 5:1–2)

GOD says that Bethlehem is *"little among the thousands of Judah,"* and so Christmas is not for the rich and the powerful. It is, rather, for the *"little"*; it is for the poor and the meek. In turn, the Bible's Christmas songs are not for the kind of glamorous people who are worshipped by the world. Rather, they are for those who are despised and rejected by the world.

There is, at Christmas, a frail, silver-haired Christian grandmother who must be wheeled into the church service in her wheelchair. There is also, at Christmas, a cheerful, ever-kind boy with Down syndrome who greets his parents and siblings with innocent bursts of jubilation just prior to the family's worship gathering in their home. At Christmas, it must not be forgotten, there is a shivering, lonely Christian prisoner of conscience, persecuted and locked up, in cruelty, caged in by concrete walls, and yearning to see the faces of his fellow church members. These are the ones for whom the Bible's Christmas songs are written.

Mary's Christmas song, for example, is not written for the rich and powerful:

Mary said,
My soul magnifies the Lord.
> *My spirit has rejoiced in God my Savior,*
> *for He has looked at **the humble state** of His servant.*
For behold, from now on, all generations will call me blessed.
> *For He who is mighty has done great things for me.*
> *Holy is His name.*
> *His mercy is for generations of generations on those*
> *who fear Him.*
He has shown strength with His arm.
> *He has scattered the proud in the imagination of their*
> *hearts.*
He has put down princes from their thrones.
> *And has **exalted the lowly**.*
He has filled the hungry with good things.
> *He has sent the rich away empty.* (Luke 1:46–53)

The shepherds of Christmas also hear a Christmas song that is not intended for the proud and mighty, but for the weak and the afflicted:

*There were **shepherds** [that is, not rich, powerful Jews, but lowly, despised Jews] in the same country staying in the field, and keeping watch by night over their flock. Behold, an angel of the Lord stood by them, and the glory of the Lord shone around them, and they were terrified. The angel said to them, "Do not be afraid, for behold, I bring you good news of great joy which will be to all the people. For there is born to you today, in [the City of David], a Savior, who is Christ the Lord. This is the sign to you: you will find a Baby wrapped in strips of cloth, **lying in a feeding trough** [i.e. He is not a comely and majestic, but a lowly, despised Babe]." Suddenly, there was with the angel a multitude of the Heavenly [host] praising God, and saying, "Glory to God in the highest, on earth peace, good will toward men." (Luke 2:8–14)*

Who, then, knows *the Bible's* Christmas songs? Who knows how to sing about Christmas in a truly *biblical* manner? With whose Christmas songs is God actually pleased?

Are we not speaking here of the Christian widow who, each and every Christmas, presses on, patiently, through her lonely pains of bereavement? Is this not the Christian son who weeps on Christmas Day for his beloved father who is languishing in prison for the sake of the Gospel? Do we not speak here of the pious Christian wife who mourns on Christmas Eve, being unable to conceive a child, despite all of her righteous prayers for a baby? Is this not the joyful Christian girl who, due to her chronic, debilitating illness, is unable to join her siblings in singing in the children's Christmas choir? Is this not the Christian janitor, mopping kitchens and scrubbing toilets, whom nobody esteems, yet who sings his hymns to God, at Christmas time, during his lonely hours of work?

THE LOWLY BIRTH OF CHRIST

The Christmas message first came to shepherds. They were not the big men of the world. They were the little men of the little town of Bethlehem. It was these shepherds, these little, nobody men living in a little, nobody town, who first heard the news about the appearance of the great Shepherd, the Messianic Shepherd whose origins are from of old:

*Now you shall gather yourself in troops, daughter of troops. He has laid siege against us. They will strike the Judge of Israel with a rod on the cheek. But you, Bethlehem Ephrathah, **being small** among the clans of Judah, out of you One will come out to Me that is to be Ruler in Israel; whose goings [forth] are from of old, from [everlasting].* (Micah 5:1–2)

THE BABES OF CHRISTMAS

The City of Bethlehem is called, by the Prophet Micah, *"Bethlehem Ephrathah."* For, the City of Bethlehem reaches back to very ancient times, to the time of Jacob and Rachel:

> *Rachel died, and was buried on the way to <u>Ephrath</u>* (**also called Bethlehem**). (Genesis 35:19)

Ephrathah was, perhaps, a family clan name. The family clan of Ephrathah lived in and around the town of Bethlehem. We know this, in part, from the book of Ruth:

> *In the days when the judges judged, there was a famine in the land. A certain man **of Bethlehem Judah** went to live in the country of Moab, he, and his wife, and his two sons. The name of the man was Elimelech, and the name of his wife Naomi. The names of his two sons were Mahlon and Chilion, <u>Ephrathites</u> of **Bethlehem Judah**. They came into the country of Moab, and lived there.* (Ruth 1:1–2)

The Ephrathites of Bethlehem were a small, nobody clan. Neither mighty, nor men of renown, they were unlikely candidates for any kingly line. Yet out of them came great royalty:

> *All the people who were in the gate, and the elders, said [to Boaz], "We are witnesses. May the* LORD *make the woman who has come into your house like Rachel and like Leah, which both built the house of Israel; and treat you worthily **in Ephrathah**, and be famous **in Bethlehem**."*

> *…and Salmon became the father of Boaz, and Boaz became the father of Obed, and Obed became the father of Jesse, and Jesse became the father **of David**.* (Ruth 4:11, 21–22)

The Prophet Micah, then, is saying that it is going to happen again! Just as King David came out of little, nobody

Bethlehem Ephrathah, so too shall the Son of David, the Messiah, come out of that little, nobody clan, and little, nobody town. Out of such a little, nobody clan, and little, nobody town, comes a great, great King.

There is, in Micah's prophecy, the crisis, the persecution, and the humble birth of the "King" of Israel. First, there is the *crisis* of the King—namely, that Israel has no king, and yet needs one ever so desperately:

> *Now why do you cry out aloud? Is there **no king** in you? Has your counselor perished, that pains have taken hold of you as of a woman in travail?* (Micah 4:9)

Secondly, there is the prophecy of the *persecution* of Israel's future King:

> *Now you shall gather yourself in troops, daughter of troops. He has laid siege against us. **They will strike the Judge of Israel with a rod on the cheek.*** (Micah 5:1)

Thirdly, Micah prophesies about the *lowly birth* of the Messiah:

> *But you, Bethlehem Ephrathah, being **small** among the clans of Judah, out of you **One** will come out to Me that is to be **Ruler** in Israel; whose goings [forth] are from of old, from [everlasting].* (Micah 5:2)

The King shall come out of *little, despised* Bethlehem Ephrathah! Most people would expect the King of kings and Lord of lords to be born in Pella, during the Greek empire, or in Rome, during the Roman empire, or at least, as a Jew, in Jerusalem. These are mighty cities, where one would expect kings to be born. But no—Jesus is born in Bethlehem. He despises the wisdom of the Greeks, the glory of Rome, and even Herod's palace at Jerusalem. Instead, He chooses the *"small"* and lowly Bethlehem.

Do you, Christian Brother or Sister, feel quite little? Do you feel unimportant? Is your little Christian clan unnoticed by the world? Are you small, and off the map? Is your little Christian church, and your *"small"* homeschool family laughed at by those whom the world calls its leaders? O precious Christian, perhaps God, in His wisdom, has made you a *"Bethlehem"* kind of family. Perhaps your little clan has indeed been chosen by God, for royal, Kingdom purposes. Neglect not the loving nurture and spiritual discipleship of your little ones. They are so much more important than you may think. They are princes and princesses in the Kingdom of God.

And just how *"small"* and despised are preborn children in our contemporary world? Do doctors really have the legal right, before God (for God's Laws are much more important than humanly crafted ones), to form and freeze human embryos through in vitro fertilization? Why do philosophers in today's universities think that preborn children have less "personhood" than post-born children? Why are so many scientists and politicians trying to redefine "life" as beginning at "implantation," rather than at conception? Are the babies who have been conceived and yet have not reached the stage of implantation any less "human" in the eyes of God? Are they too *"small"* to be given the status of God's image bearers, and too tiny to be loved by the Lord of Hosts? Or are these pre-implantation babies—the ones who are so cruelly murdered through an array of abortifacient contraceptives[1]—extremely important to God? Are they not *"Bethlehem"* babies?

---

[1] Such murderous contraceptives include the birth control pill, the so-called "morning after pill," intrauterine devices (or "IUD's"), and other drugs/devices that can, in some instances, inhibit the implantation of a newly-conceived baby in the womb. See *Divine Heartbeat*, 16n27, 17n29.

CHRIST, THE ANCIENT BABE

Yet there is much more to the prophecy, since the Prophet Micah is speaking of an *ancient* King. He, the King who shall come out of little Bethlehem Ephrathah, is from *ancient times past*:

> *But you, Bethlehem Ephrathah, being small among the clans of Judah, out of you One will come out to Me that is to be Ruler in Israel;* ***whose goings [forth] are from of old,*** *from [everlasting].* (Micah 5:2)

"From of old" could mean, possibly, "from ancient human history." For, in the days of Nehemiah, the worship ordinances of David and Asaph are said to be *"in the days of old"*:

> *They performed the duty of their God, and the duty of the purification, and so did the singers and the porters, according to the commandment of David, and of Solomon his son. For* ***in the days*** *of David and Asaph* ***of old*** *there was a chief of the singers, and songs of praise and thanksgiving to God.* (Nehemiah 12:45–46)

However, in Micah's prophecy about the coming Ruler, He is not only *"from of old,"* but also *"from everlasting"*: *"...whose goings [forth] are from of old,* ***from [everlasting]"*** (Micah 5:2c). This is ineffably grand, for, in the Bible, it is God alone whose *"goings forth"* are more ancient than human history, itself (that is, God is eternal, without beginning or end). God is the only rightful King of kings, and God is not merely from ancient times. He, the Lord God, is from the *eternal* past:

*The **eternal** God is your dwelling place.*
*Underneath are the **everlasting** arms.*[2]
He thrust out the enemy from before you,
and said, "Destroy!" (Deuteronomy 33:27)

Also,

*Yet God is my King **of old**,*
working salvation throughout the earth. (Psalm 74:12)

Who, then, is Jesus? Are His origins in Nazareth? Or are they, rather, in Bethlehem? And are they merely in Bethlehem, or also, in some wondrous way, actually preceding Bethlehem? Are not His *"goings [forth]…from of old, from [everlasting]"*?

Even Jesus' enemies knew that His origins were mysterious. His ancestry was obscure. Joseph was not His biological father. They blamed this on fornication:

*They said to Him, "We were not **born of sexual immorality**. We have one Father, God."* (John 8:41)

---

[2] The Hebrew of Deuteronomy 33:27 has a breathtaking parallel with Micah 5:2. It is hard to think that Micah did not have Deuteronomy 33:27 at the forefront of his mind when he, by the perfect inspiration of the Holy Spirit, penned Micah 5:2. For, in Hebrew, the *"eternal"* term in Deuteronomy 33:27 is the exact same term as Micah's *"of old"* term in Micah 5:2 (the Hebrew *qédem* underlies both English terms), while the word *"everlasting"* in Deuteronomy 33:27 is the same Hebrew word (*'ôlām*) as the one that underlies Micah's use of *"everlasting"* in Micah 5:2. The parallel can be presented in English as follows:

The <u>of-old</u> God is your dwelling place,
Underneath are the <u>everlasting</u> arms. (Deuteronomy 33:27)

Whose going outs are from <u>of old</u>,
From <u>everlasting</u>. (Micah 5:2)

The truth, however, is that Jesus' origins are not to be found in pre-marital sexual sin. Mary was a virgin when she conceived. This miraculous conception was from God — Mary being overshadowed by the Holy Spirit — not from man. Fully Man, Jesus was indeed born of Mary. Yet she was a virgin. And so His origins are mysteriously wonderful:

*Therefore He will abandon them until the time that **she who is in labor gives birth**. Then the rest of His brothers will return to the children of Israel.* (Micah 5:3)

Who is *"she who is in labor"* who *"gives birth"*? Is this not the virgin, who is Mary? Why, then, must she be a virgin? Is it not because her Son's origins are from of old, from everlasting?

*But you, Bethlehem Ephrathah, being small among the clans of Judah, out of you One will come out to Me that is to be Ruler in Israel; **whose goings [forth] are from of old, from [everlasting]**.* (Micah 5:2)

When did Christ originate? What marked the beginning of His existence? He had no beginning. There never was a time when He was not. Before the creation of the universe, He was. Before all time and space, He eternally WAS:

The Jews therefore said to Him, "You are not yet fifty years old, and have you seen Abraham?"

*Jesus said to them, "Most certainly, I tell you, **before Abraham came into existence, I AM**."* (John 8:57–58)

We are little people. We are *"Bethlehem"* kind of people, being quite small and despised by the world. Yet we remember, with worshipful trembling, that out of Bethlehem came forth the Messianic Babe. He, our Lord Jesus, is the

Babe who preceded us, and preceded all of humanity, eternally. He is the *ancient* Babe. His origins are from of old, from everlasting. He has no beginning. He shall have no end. Before time began, HE WAS. At the present, HE IS. When He returns, HE SHALL BE. The Messianic Babe of Christmas has an *eternal* Kingship.

As a professing Christian, a man finds himself talking to a Mormon acquaintance. At the end of their highly religious discussion and debate, the Mormon says, "Well, we don't need to say that one of us is wrong. We both believe in Jesus. We both believe that Jesus died on the cross to save us from our sins. That's all that matters." Now, if the professing Christian is a member of today's compromised church, he will find this Mormon line of ecumenical thought not entirely easy to answer.[3] For the truncated, doctrine-deficient "gospel" of the compromised church no longer knows how to distinguish, with decisive conviction, between Christian orthodoxy and outright heresy.

How, then, would a God-fearing, historic Christian answer such a Mormon ecumenical challenge? Would he press Mormon definitions of *"faith"* and *"works"* until the Mormon man in question is exasperated at the logical hair-splitting that would necessarily be involved? No, the historic Christian would aim right at the heart of the matter. He would ask his Mormon acquaintance, "Did the Son of God

---

[3] The present author, while living in Utah, has spoken, personally, to several Mormon missionaries who vehemently professed "salvation by grace alone, through faith alone, in Christ alone." Whether or not these missionaries were anomalies to Mormonism is beside the point. The point is that the formula "salvation by grace alone, through faith alone, in Christ alone" is an insufficient litmus test for the totality of true Christianity. It may test well for the doctrine of justification by faith, but it leaves plenty of room for apostatizing heresies regarding other historic doctrines of our faith that pertain directly to our salvation. For example, one could affirm this "grace alone, faith alone, Christ alone" formula and, simultaneously, deny, outright, the doctrine of the Trinity.

have a beginning? Was there a time when Christ, the Father's Son, was not?"

Then, as the Mormon acquaintance would have to reply, if he were honest, "Well, yes, the Son of God did have a beginning, but we both believe that we must be saved by faith in Jesus' death for our sins, so..." the historic Christian would politely interject by declaring that they are not speaking together of the same "Jesus." To wit, a Jesus Christ who "had a beginning" is a false Jesus, a demonic version of "Jesus." For, the Jesus Christ of historic Christianity, of the Scriptures, has no beginning. To say otherwise is Idolatry, in the capital "I" sense of the word. Therefore, this Mormon man is not talking about the same God as the God of biblical faith. Thus he is not talking about the same Gospel as the Gospel of historic Christianity—which is the only Gospel by which one may be saved.

Sound doctrine is vital to Christmas. (Bad doctrine seeks to murder and destroy Christmas.) For, God did not *create* His Son in Mary's womb. The Son of God was *never created*. The Son of God is *eternally uncreated*. This is sound doctrine, and Christmas cannot exist without it.

In Mary's womb, the Son of God *assumed*, or *took on* a human nature. Yet the Son of God remained uncreated, even in Mary's womb. This means that He possessed, in Mary's womb, both a full human nature, and a full divine nature, without mixing the natures, confusing the natures, or replacing the natures. Jesus Christ is not half-God, half-human, nor is He a divine mind poured into a human shell. Nor is He two "Persons," one of human and one of God. Rather, Jesus Christ is fully God and fully human, *one eternal Person, existing in two distinct natures*.

Herein lies the mystery, wonder, and joyful fear of Christmas. It is found not in the cinematic dazzle of existentialist or postmodern Christmas films, but in the plain, humble writings of the Church Fathers (that is, only insofar as they reflect accurately upon the Holy Scriptures).

The wonder of Christmas is this: the *eternal* Son of God took on *finite* humanity, while still remaining *infinite*! The *incorruptible* Son of God took on *corruptible* humanity, while still remaining *incorruptible*! The *everlasting* Son of God entered into our own *temporal* world, with human baby toes and human baby tears, while still remaining *everlasting* in His divine nature. He is the *eternally ancient* Babe.[4]

Who, then, would be so mad as to question the "Personhood" of the Babe in Mary's womb, from conception onwards? Did the pre-implantation Babe in Mary's womb lack Personhood? To say so would be to commit an unthinkable heresy. For, the newly conceived Babe in Mary's womb was the eternally ancient Son of God. He Himself, Christ our Lord, establishes, through His incarnation, full "Personhood" in the womb, from conception onwards. Therefore, let no man assert that the "personhood" of any baby in the womb may be called into question, from conception onwards.

Christ Jesus, the Babe in Mary's womb, is the eternally ancient Babe. Come, then, you who know and fear the Lord. Come let us worship and bow down before *Him*, the ancient Babe, this Christmas.

---

[4] Consider here the wondrous, poetic prose of Gregory of Nazianzus (c. 330-390) on the truthful, historical mysteries of Christmas: "He whom presently you scorn was once transcendent, over even you. He who is presently human was incomposite. He remained what He was; what He was not, He assumed. No 'because' is required for His existence in the beginning, for what could account for the existence of God? …He was begotten—yet He was already [eternally] begotten—of a woman. And yet she was a virgin. That it was from a woman makes it human, that she was a virgin makes it divine. On earth He has no father, but in Heaven no mother.…He was wrapped in swaddling bands, but at the Resurrection He unloosed the swaddling bands of the grave" (Gregory of Nazianzus, *The Five Theological Orations* 29:19 [trans. Lionel Wickham; New York: St. Vladimir's Seminary Press, 2002], 86-87).

THE ANCIENT BABE IS ALSO THE MAJESTIC SHEPHERD

There are two more things to be said about this ancient King—this ancient Babe in Micah 5. The first is that He is also a *majestic Shepherd*. He will grow up to *shepherd* Israel in the *majesty* of the name of the Lord:

*Therefore He will abandon them until the time that she who is in labor gives birth. Then the rest of His brothers will return to the children of Israel. He shall stand, and **shall shepherd** in the strength of the LORD, in the **majesty** of the name of the LORD His God: and they will live, for then He will be great to the ends of the earth. He will be our peace when Assyria invades our land, and when he marches through our fortresses, then we will raise against him seven shepherds, and eight leaders of men.* (Micah 5:3–5)

In ancient Israel, kings are "shepherds." To be the king of a nation is to be the shepherd of that nation:

*...from following the ewes that have their young, He brought [David] to be **the shepherd** of Jacob, His people, and Israel, His inheritance. So he was their **shepherd** according to the integrity of his heart, and guided them by the skillfulness of his hands.* (Psalm 78:71–72)

In the fifth chapter of Micah, the Babe grows up to be the Shepherd of Israel. This royal, Messianic Babe is, therefore, not only an ancient Babe, but also a majestic Shepherd:

*He shall stand, and **shall shepherd** in the strength of the LORD, in the **majesty** of the name of the LORD His God: and they will live, for then He will be great to the ends of the earth.* (Micah 5:4)

The ancient Babe grows up to *shepherd* Israel in the strength of the Lord, in the *majesty* of the Lord's name. He is thus a majestic Shepherd. And this is divine truth, for in the Old Testament, *God* is a majestic Shepherd over His people Israel. As such, in the Old Testament, God is wrathful to destroy the enemies of Israel, and yet quick to bring the joy of salvation to His people:

*Hear us, **O Shepherd of Israel**, You who lead Joseph like a flock, You who sit above the cherubim, shine out.* (Psalm 80:1)

The Lord is Israel's Shepherd, and He shepherds her in majesty by pouring out His wrath upon her enemies:

*In the greatness of **Your [majesty]**, You overthrow those who rise up against You. You send out **Your wrath**. It consumes them as stubble.* (Exodus 15:7)

Also,

*Men shall go into the caves of the rocks, and into the holes of the earth, from before **the terror of the LORD**, and from **the glory of His majesty**, when He arises to shake the earth mightily. In that day, men shall cast away their idols of silver, and their idols of gold, which have been made for themselves to worship, to the moles and to the bats; to go into the caverns of the rocks, and into the clefts of the ragged rocks, from before **the terror of the LORD**, and from **the glory of His majesty**, when He arises to shake the earth mightily.* (Isaiah 2:19–21)

At the same time, God, as a majestic Shepherd, brings great salvation and joy to His people, who fear Him:

*These shall lift up their voice. They will shout for **the majesty of the LORD**. They cry aloud from the sea.* (Isaiah 24:14)

Thus in the Old Testament, God, as a majestic Shepherd, brings both wrath upon His enemies and saving joy to His children. The same is true in the New Testament:

*The kings of the earth, the princes, the commanding officers, the rich, the strong, and every slave and free person, hid themselves in the caves and in the rocks of the mountains. They told the mountains and the rocks, "Fall on us, and hide us from the face of Him who sits on the throne, and from **the wrath of the Lamb**, for **the great day of His wrath** has come; and who is able to stand?"* (Revelation 6:15–17)

The ancient Babe grows up to become the majestic Shepherd. The little Lamb of Christmas grows up to execute wrath upon the nations who terrify His people. He executes *"the wrath of the Lamb."* Yet this wrathful Lamb also rules as the majestic Shepherd over His elect. In doing so, He brings to them the joy of His salvation:

*They will never be hungry, neither thirsty anymore; neither will the sun beat on them, nor any heat; for **the Lamb** who is in the middle of the throne **shepherds them**, and leads them to springs of waters of life. And God will wipe away every tear from their eyes.* (Revelation 7:16–17)

We want to worship the Babe of Christmas. In seeking Him in the Scriptures, we find the Prophet Micah describing Him to us as an eternally ancient Babe — He is God with us — who grows up to become a majestic Shepherd. In turn, His role as the majestic Shepherd grants Him the authority to pour out the fullness of His wrath upon the wicked. It also bestows upon Him the honor of pouring out the fullness of His joy upon the righteous. The Babe of Christmas will grow up to shepherd the nations in His wrathful, yet salvific righteousness.

Is there, then, any room today in our churches and homes for the *majestic Shepherd* of Christmas? Are churches today still allowed to talk about the wrath of God against the wicked at Christmas time, or has the American "prosperity Gospel" excommunicated the majestic Shepherd, as the Prophet Micah reveals Him to us, from His own Christmas celebration? Are our children aware of the majesty of the Shepherd whom we follow, like little lambs, at Christmas time? Do our children know how to tremble before Him, with godly, joyful fear, during the Christmas season?[5] Have they been taught by their pastors and parents how to warn others of the coming wrath of the Lamb, even at Christmas time, or, better put, especially at Christmas time?[6]

THE ANCIENT BABE SHALL BE THE VICTORIOUS SHEPHERD

The second thing that must be said about this ancient Babe of the fifth chapter of Micah, this Babe who shall grow into the *majestic Shepherd*, is that He also will become a *victorious Shepherd*. He not only shall be *majestic* with His Shepherd's staff; He also shall be *victorious* with it. In specific, He shall be victorious over the land of Nimrod:

---

[5] The present author is in no way opposed to the *joyful* singing of doctrinally sound Christmas hymns at Christmas time. It is to be a season of great, God-centered joy. He simply reminds the Church that Isaac Watts, in his "Joy to the World" Christmas hymn, keeps reverence for Christ in the midst of the celebration. For, in Watts' hymn, Christ Jesus "makes the nations prove the glories of His righteousness." Also, the present author heartily recommends the singing of Christmas hymns such as "Let All Mortal Flesh Keep Silence," which balance the joy of our salvation, marked by the birth of the Lamb of God, with deep reverence for the dreadful majesty of our Christmas Shepherd.

[6] For, does not the celebration of Christ's First Advent prompt us to reflect, with fear and trembling, upon His Second Advent? And as we are duty-bound by the Gospel to announce, boldly, His First Advent, are we not also obligated, by obedience and love towards God, to proclaim, unashamedly, the certain approach of His Second Advent?

*He will be our peace when Assyria invades our land, and when he marches through our fortresses, then we will raise against him seven shepherds, and eight leaders of men. They will rule **the land of Assyria** with the sword, and **the land of Nimrod** in its gates. He will deliver us from the Assyrian, when he invades our land, and when he marches within our border.* (Micah 5:5–6)

Nimrod was an ancient foe. According to the tenth chapter of Genesis, he was, in his day, the strongest enemy of the people of God, and he founded the civilization that grew into the Kingdom of Assyria.[7] It makes much sense, then, that *"the land of Nimrod"* is named by Micah as the land from whom the coming Shepherd will deliver Israel. For, in Micah's own day, Assyria was Israel's strongest and most terrifying enemy. Joyfully, then, the ancient Babe of Micah's prophecy shall grow up and become the majestic Shepherd over Israel, and He, the Shepherd, shall be *victorious* over Assyria:

He will be our peace when Assyria invades our land, *and when he marches through our fortresses, then we will raise against him seven shepherds, and eight leaders of men. They will rule the land of Assyria with the sword, and the land of Nimrod in its gates.* **He will deliver us from the Assyrian,** *when he invades our land, and when he marches within our border.* (Micah 5:5–6)

---

[7] Nimrod is a descendent of Noah's son Ham, being the grandson of Ham through Ham's son, Cush (Genesis 10:8). His name may mean, "We shall rebel," stemming from the Hebrew verb *mārad*, or else "he rebels." He is described as a *"mighty-warrior hunter"* (v. 9), and may well have "hunted" men, with oppressive violence, as much as he hunted animals. Nimrod began his evil kingdom at Babel (v. 10), and later became the founder and builder of the city of Nineveh, in Assyria (v. 11).

This is good news! This ancient Babe, *"whose goings [forth] are from of old, from [everlasting]"* (Micah 5:2c), shall come to Israel, being born of a woman, and when He comes to Israel He shall deliver His people from their strongest enemies. Assyria shall be driven back and conquered. Eventually, even Rome shall fall and be destroyed.

Of course, there is an enemy much greater than Assyria, and even mightier than Rome. It is the kingdom of Sin and Death. Satan is the ruler of this kingdom, and we were, formerly, its subjects. But thanks be to God, through Christ Jesus our Lord, the *victorious* Shepherd, that we have been liberated from this awful kingdom. Jesus, *the Victor*, has shed His blood for us on the cross. The Good Shepherd has laid down His life for His sheep. He died the wrathful death that we deserved. He was slaughtered with the slaughter that our sins demanded of us. Therefore, He has conquered Sin and Death, our greatest foes! He is risen from the dead. Thus He is, to be sure, a most *victorious* Shepherd!

Yet what is striking in Micah's prophecy is the manner with which the Shepherd, this *victorious* Shepherd, brings about His complete victory over Assyria. Namely, He employs sub-shepherds, or under-shepherds to finish His conquest of His enemies:

> *He will be our peace when Assyria invades our land, and when he marches through our fortresses,* **then we will raise against him seven shepherds, and eight leaders of men.** *They will rule the land of Assyria with the sword, and the land of Nimrod in its gates. He will deliver us from the Assyrian, when he invades our land, and when he marches within our border.* (Micah 5:5–6)

The ancient Babe grows up to become the *victorious* Shepherd, *by Himself*, to be sure. Yet He chooses, in His sovereign will, to employ under-shepherds to finish His war against Assyria. They, the under-shepherds, will rule over

Assyria with the sword. They shall execute the vengeance of God with the sword in their hands. And, in a spiritual sense,[8] this is not unlike the under-shepherds of the New Testament Church. Yet they, the pastors, "rule" as "servants," and their only sword is the *Sword of the Spirit, which is the Word of God*" (Ephesians 6:17). They are sub-shepherds under the Chief-Shepherd-hood of Christ:

> *I exhort the elders among you, as a fellow elder, and a witness of the sufferings of Christ, and who will also share in the glory that will be revealed.* **Shepherd the flock of God which is among you,** *exercising the oversight, not under compulsion, but voluntarily, not for dishonest gain, but willingly; neither as lording it over those entrusted to you, but making yourselves examples to the flock.* **When the Chief Shepherd is revealed,** *you will receive the crown of glory that does not fade away.* (1 Peter 5:1–4)

Where, then, are the under-shepherds of God's flock when it comes to the protection of children in the womb? Why are so many pastors today in favor of contraception, when John Chrysostom, one of the greatest under-shepherds that the Church has ever known, called it a murderous practice?[9] Also, why are pastors today more concerned about their "church membership numbers" and personal paychecks than about preaching, forthrightly and uncompromisingly, towards the total abolition of abortion in our world? Surely, it must be the case that such men do not expect the Chief Shepherd to reward them with the honors of true under-shepherds in His eternal Kingdom. For if they do carry this expectation in their hearts, are they not

---

[8] Of course, the doctrine of the Millennial Kingdom of Christ foresees a literal, physical fulfillment of this prophecy, also.

[9] For the reason why Chrysostom viewed even non-abortifacient contraceptives as "murderous," see *Divine Heartbeat*, 35-36.

deceiving themselves even more than they are deceiving others?

Jesus Christ, the *victorious* Shepherd, who has defeated Satan, sin, and death by His one, decisive blow of resurrection from the grave, mysteriously chooses to finish His war against His enemies by employing other shepherds—under-shepherds. That is, His pastors, along with the deacons and church members who are under their pastoral care, have been given the task of laying waste with the sword the spiritual Assyria of this world. Yet these are not physical swords with which His pastors fight. Rather, as the under-shepherds who belong to the *victorious* Shepherd, today's pastors (and those who are under their care) fight and win by their own sufferings and martyrdoms:

> *There was war in the sky. Michael and his angels made war on the dragon. The dragon and his angels made war. They did not prevail, neither was a place found for him any more in heaven. The great dragon was thrown down, the old serpent, he who is called the devil and Satan, the deceiver of the whole world. He was thrown down to the earth, and his angels were thrown down with him. I heard a loud voice in heaven, saying, "Now the salvation, the power, and the Kingdom of our God, and the authority of his Christ has come; for the accuser of our brothers has been thrown down, who accuses them before our God day and night. They overcame him [through the blood of the Lamb], and [through] of the word of their testimony. They did not love their life, even to death.* (Revelation 12:7–11)

Precious Reader, are you suffering greatly this Christmas? Is Christmas a time of great tribulation for you this year? Are you being persecuted? Or, are you grieving, such that the shadows of death seem to have fallen upon you this Christmas? Do you feel that the ancient Babe of Christmas, who grew up to become the majestic, victorious Shepherd of Micah's prophecy, has all but forgotten you?

If so, could it not be, beloved Reader, that He, the victorious Shepherd, is actually conquering souls and defeating Satan through your sufferings? Could it not be that the death that you feel within your members is bringing life to others? Is it not possible that your smallness and weakness is making room for His greatness and His strength? As the world belittles you, is not His glory magnified? Could it not be that the more you feel like Bethlehem Ephrathah, despised and hated by the world, the more Christ is formed in you, and the more Christ shall be preached to the world?

Are you a hurt and wounded sheep? Then, does not the majestic Shepherd know how to heal your wounds with the medicine of eternal life? Are you a hunted and slaughtered sheep? Then, is not the victorious Shepherd strong enough to raise you out of death, and to destroy the very enemies that attack you?

And who better than the ancient Babe, who grew up to become Israel's majestic, victorious Shepherd, knows how to feel, with fullness of heart, the plight of preborn children at Christmas time? For the preborn, the "land of Nimrod" is everywhere. Not only in Islamic countries (where they will not be aborted, legally, but will, most likely, be coerced into the antichrist-worship of Allah even in early childhood), but in all of the nations of the world they are very vulnerable. China's murderous anti-procreation policies loom over the delicate heads of preborn children. Global powers such as the United Kingdom, the United States, and even the State of Israel continue to preach against the horrors of Nazi Germany, while at the same time using abortifacients and surgical abortions in such vast numbers as to dwarf Nazi Germany in its atrocities. Yet the One who came, previously, as the ancient Babe, shall return to earth as the majestic, victorious Shepherd. When He does, He shall strike "the land of Nimrod" with the rod of His mouth, and He shall slay the wicked of the earth with the breath of His lips.

The ancient Babe grew up to become Israel's Shepherd. He who was from the eternal past entered into time and space so that He could reveal the majesty of God to us, and bring the victory of God to us. He is, therefore, worthy to be our eternal Shepherd. He who, as the ancient Babe, the ancient Lamb, who is *"the Lamb slain from the foundation of the world"* (Revelation 3:8, KJV), offered His own blood for the blotting out of our sins, is risen from the grave, and thus is worthy to be our Shepherd. He shall be our God, and we shall be His people; we shall be His lambs, and He shall be our Shepherd.

In Heaven, then, we who know and fear God will be like lambs, leaping for joy. Also, in Heaven, the babies of the Abortion Holocaust shall be raised from the dead, immortal and imperishable. They, too, shall be in the Shepherd's fold. They shall, in fact, be amongst His most prized little lambs. And there, in the Father's good Land, we, together with them, shall be led to fountains of living water by our Good Shepherd — who was once the ancient Babe of Christmas — whose goings forth are from of old, from everlasting. Amen.

Part Two:

The Kingdom Babes

THE BABES OF CHRISTMAS

4

THE JOYFUL BABE:
John the Baptist and Preborn Children

(Luke 1:39-45)

*Mary arose in those days and went into the hill country with
haste, into a city of Judah, and entered into the house of Zacharias
and greeted Elizabeth. When Elizabeth heard Mary's greeting, the
baby leaped in her womb, and Elizabeth was filled with the Holy
Spirit. She called out with a loud voice, and said, "Blessed are you
among women, and blessed is the fruit of your womb! Why am I so
favored, that the mother of my Lord should come to me? For
behold, when the voice of your greeting came into my ears, the
baby leaped in my womb for joy! Blessed is she who believed, for
there will be a fulfillment of the things which have been spoken to
her from the Lord!" (Luke 1:39-45)*

GOD has made women to be mothers.[1] In the Bible, there
is an inseparable, unbreakable bond between the nature of
womanhood and the calling of motherhood. Yet women of
the Church who fear God, and who thus know this to be
true, oftentimes, upon hearing this truth proclaimed in the
Church, are subjected to a piercing pain in their hearts. For,
there are many mothers in the Church who have been
bereaved of their children. Also, there are not a few single
women in the Church who long to marry a God-fearing
man, and to become mothers through Christian marriage,

---

[1] Much of the biblical content of this present chapter is adapted from
Chapter 10 of *Divine Heartbeat*, 195-218, entitled "The Baby Leaped!
Elizabeth, Mary, and Preborn Children." However, as evidenced by this
opening paragraph, many of the specific lines of thought and
applications of the biblical material are unique to this present chapter.

but who have not yet had their longing fulfilled. Not only that, but there are also many married women in the Church who have suffered for years, if not decades, under the sharp, prolonged pains of a barren womb.[2] Lastly, there are certainly many women in the Church who possess a special calling from the Lord to Christian chastity. These single women — fully chaste and fully dedicated to the work of the Lord — being some of God's most special servants, are nevertheless wrongly undervalued by others in the Church on account of their chaste, unmarried, non-motherly status.

Still, the axiom remains true: God has made women for motherhood. All Christian women are called by God to be mothers. Many are called to biological motherhood within the safe confines of a God-fearing marriage (1 Timothy 5:14). Some of those who carry a cross of barrenness are called to adoptive motherhood, in light of God's love and care for the orphan (Psalm 68:5; 146:9; James 1:27). Still other women, either barren or single, are called to devote themselves fully to the Lord and, in the process, become fruitful "spiritual mothers" — which is an everlasting form of motherhood — in their discipleship of other women through their labors in the work of the Gospel (1 Corinthians 7:34).[3]

---

[2] Such courageous Christian married women have rejected the *sinfully abhorrent* practices of artificial insemination and in vitro fertilization.

[3] Let it be said in our increasingly feminist age that the Lord does not permit women to be pastors and deacons in His Church (1 Timothy 3:2; 3:12), nor does He allow them to preach from the pulpit (1 Timothy 2:12). He also permits them neither to be heads of state, nor to be legislators of state (such as Members of Parliament, Congress, Senate, etc.), since God designed men, and not women, to bear the fierce, combative, battle-heavy tasks of governing the state (Deuteronomy 1:13-15; Isaiah 3:12). However, this in no way diminishes the eternal importance of the motherly, helping, nurturing, and yet still *submissive* roles of women's ministry and women's evangelistic endeavors assigned to the women of the Church in their various callings of "spiritual motherhood" (2 Kings 22:14; Luke 8:2-3; Acts 9:36; 21:9; Romans 16:1-15; Philippians 4:2-3; etc.).

Yet this is a very despised axiom in our society. For, today's world is captivated by psychological theories (which are, at core, demonic theories) about some women being born with unchangeable "lesbian identities," while other women are said to be born with immutable "transgender identities."[4] Moreover, the very tenets of modern feminism advocate a strong separation between femininity and motherhood. Moses' mother triumphed over Egypt when she *"nursed"* her baby boy (Exodus 2:9). Yet modern feminism labors to create a "bottle-fed" culture, since it sees the bottle as a vehicle of "liberation" from stay-at-home motherhood (in direct defiance of God's wise and loving, *"Be...workers at home"* command given to Christian mothers in Titus 2:5).

No doubt, it is true, as modern feminism loves to point out, that throughout world history, women have been mistreated and oppressed by men in multitudinous and nefarious ways. In response to this, we may mention that the modern feminist retelling of this horrible history purposefully neglects the seemingly countless and certainly diabolical ways in which women have seduced, manipulated, displaced, tormented, and even murdered men. Still, the historical truth of men's tyrannical acts over women must not be forgotten. Being of the weaker gender,

---

[4] Yet the authoritative Word of God, which cannot be broken, says that the nature of woman is distinctly, inconfusedly feminine. For example, a woman's dress must be distinctly feminine, else it make her an abomination to the Lord (Deuteronomy 22:5; 1 Corinthians 11:1-16). Also, Romans 1:26 says this of the sinful abomination of lesbianism: *"For this reason, God gave them up to vile passions. For their women changed the natural function into that which is against nature."*

women, more often than not, have been forced by men into a very lowly societal status.[5]

Elizabeth and Mary are two *women* at the very heart of the Christmas account. It is the faith of these two women, juxtaposed with the doubting heart of Elizabeth's husband, Zacharias, that ushers in the triumph of the Christmas events. Just as Jesus' first resurrection appearances were to women, rather than men (Matthew 28:9; Mark 16:9; John 20:14), so too does the historical account in Luke emphasize the victory of these women's faith at the very beginnings of the Messiah's Advent. For, while Zacharias, the man, *"did not believe"* the words of the Angel Gabriel, it was Mary, the woman, who truly *"believed"* Gabriel's glad tidings:

> THE ANGEL GABRIEL TO ZACHARIAS: *"Behold, you will be silent and not able to speak, until the day that these things will happen, because **you did not believe** my words, which will be fulfilled in their proper time."* (Luke 1:20)

> ELIZABETH TO MARY: *"Blessed is **she who believed**, for there will be a fulfillment of the things which have been spoken to her from the Lord!"* (Luke 1:45)

Yet the triumph of Elizabeth and Mary is the very opposite of what one might call a "modern feminist triumph." These pious women do, indeed, triumph over the historic, oppressive sins that men have so brutally committed against women. Yet their triumph is of the distinctly God-fearing type. That is, they are victorious

---

[5] Christian husbands, therefore, have a wonderful opportunity to demonstrate the Gospel's undoing of this history of women's oppression by men. For example, Christian husbands can take their spiritual headship in marriage and, following Ephesians 5:25-27, use it to demonstrate their sacrificial, servant-natured love for their wives. They can, for instance, become the primary toilet cleaners in the home!

through humility, not self-exaltation. Elizabeth and Mary triumph not through usurpation of male authority, but *through the glory of female submission*, under God. What is more, they are victorious not through economic and political empowerment, but rather through their obedience to the biblical command of godly procreation. They triumph *through the distinctly feminine glory of child bearing!* As the blessed Apostle says:

> *...but* **she will be saved through her childbearing**, *if they continue in faith, love, and sanctification with sobriety.* (1 Timothy 2:15)

What is the glory of woman? Is it not her submissive posture before God, her Protector and Provider? The Apostle says, *"But if a woman has long hair, it is a glory to her, for her hair is given to her for a covering"* (1 Corinthians 11:15). Therefore, what is admirable in a married woman is her faithful act of submitting herself under the headship of God, and, after being first under God, also submitting herself under the headship of her husband. Moreover, procreation makes a married woman admirable. This is her glory and crown. For, *"...she will be saved through her childbearing."*

Thus despite what many political conservatives might think, Margaret Thatcher, Prime Minister of the United Kingdom from 1979-1990, was not an admirable woman. For, she usurped God's standards of male headship in political office, championed her own personal use of contraception in the name of political expediency,[6] and

---

[6] See "Lady Thatcher's Private Life Laid Bare by Gorman," *The Telegraph* (October 24, 2001), n.p. [cited April 13, 2015]. Online: http://www.telegraph.co.uk/comment/4266424/Lady-Thatchers-private-life-laid-bare-by-Gorman.html.

equivocated on abortion.[7] She is thus nowhere near to being the God-fearing, quintessential female role model that today's greatly confused Christian women so desperately need.

Who, then, is a worthy personage for being such an admirable, feminine role model? In today's upside-down culture, wherein women shun their God-created, feminine glory in search of the forbidden fruit of a more masculine, or even genderless glory, to whom shall real Christian women look for godly imitation on womanhood?

There is, most graciously, an exemplary Jewish woman whose humble personage God has preserved for us in the Bible. She is a woman whose feminine glory and crown—that of childbearing—has been withheld from her, by divine providence. Being gray-haired, she is nevertheless barren, and childless. Yet she remains faithful, quiet, and submissive to God. She thus embodies many of the quintessential virtues of womanhood, even as she suffers under one of the worst pains of womanhood—that of barrenness. She is a true woman, in the biblical sense. Yet she is also a true sufferer under her true womanhood. Therefore, God chooses to visit her with a miraculous conception, and commands that her son be given the name John.

ELIZABETH'S BABE IS *ELIZABETH'S* BABE

It is not only that Elizabeth is *John's* mother. It is also that John is *Elizabeth's* son. That is, many envious women would marvel at the high privilege of being John's mother. Yet the truth is most likely that John, in his humility,

---

[7] For Thatcher's equivocation on abortion, see John Smeaton, "Baroness Thatcher's Voting Record on Pro-life and Pro-family Issues," *John Smeaton SPUC Director* (April 18, 2013), n.p. [cited April 13, 2015]. Online: http://spuc-director.blogspot.co.uk/2013/04/baroness-thatchers-voting-record-on-pro.html.

marveled at the wonder of being Elizabeth's son. For, her spiritual greatness preceded his own.

The Suffering Faith of Elizabeth

Yet Elizabeth's greatness is not "greatness" according to the world's measurements. It is, rather, a greatness of faith achieved through an immeasurable amount of suffering:

> *There was in the days of Herod, the king of Judea, a certain priest named Zacharias, of the priestly division of Abijah. He had a wife of the daughters of Aaron, and her name was Elizabeth. They were both **righteous before God**, walking blamelessly in all the commandments and ordinances of the Lord. But they had no child, because Elizabeth **was barren**, and they both were **well advanced in years**.* (Luke 1:5-7)

How can this be? If God has taken special note of Zacharias and Elizabeth as being *"righteous before [Him],"* how can Elizabeth be marked out by His providence for the lifelong pain of barrenness? Is not barrenness typically seen as a curse in the Old Testament, and does not righteousness guard one from barrenness in the Old Testament?

> *No one will miscarry or be barren in your land. I will fulfill the number of your days.* (Exodus 23:26)

Elizabeth, then, is much like righteous Job. She is more righteous than others, yet she simultaneously appears to be more cursed than others. As a result, she suffers a deep reproach under the condemning gaze of her own people. Thus she also shares in the sufferings of Hannah, who likewise was barren, and who likewise was scornfully reproached in her barrenness:

*She was **in bitterness of soul**, and prayed to the LORD, **weeping bitterly**.* (1 Samuel 1:10)

More than this, Elizabeth is scorned by her own family members for giving her son the name John. The Lord has commanded Zacharias and Elizabeth to name him John, but their relatives are upset with this uncustomary Christening:

*They said to her, **"There is no one among your relatives who is called by this name."*** (Luke 1:61)

We must be careful not to read too much into this (somewhat mild) extended-family persecution, and yet we cannot help but wonder if it is a foreshadowing of the persecutions that John will have to face when he grows up. For, just as his extended family rejected his God-ordained name, so too shall most of his national family (the children of Abraham) reject his God-ordained preaching. Or, to put it another way, Elizabeth's naming of John violates extended-family traditions for the sake of God's Word, just as John's preaching will violate the "family traditions" of Israel for the sake of God's Word:

*He said therefore to the multitudes who went out to be baptized by him, "You offspring of vipers, who warned you to flee from the wrath to come? Therefore produce fruits worthy of repentance, and do not begin to say among yourselves, 'We have Abraham for our father'; for I tell you that **God is able to raise up children to Abraham from these stones**!"* (Luke 3:7–8)

Where, then, does John the Baptist learn how to suffer so patiently for the Gospel of Christ? He learns this from his suffering mother. She who has suffered so much in the hot, refining fires of God's providence is able to train her son how to be the suffering messenger who will prepare the way for the coming of the Refiner's Fire, Himself.

Elizabeth's Bible-centered Faith

We notice, next, that Elizabeth, along with Zacharias, is very much capable of teaching the boy John vast amounts of biblical knowledge. For, just as deep suffering for the sake of righteousness qualifies a mother to prepare her son for a life of such suffering, so too does deep knowledge of God's Scriptures qualify her to train her son to be a man of the Scriptures. And Elizabeth is such a mother. She has a Bible-saturated mind, and a Bible-centered faith. Thus she is uniquely qualified to train her son in the Scriptures.

It is breathtaking to get a glimpse of the vastness of Elizabeth's pious knowledge of the Bible. For example, after she comes to realize her miraculous pregnancy, she responds with a statement of gratitude towards God:

*"Thus has the Lord done to me in the days in which He looked at me, **to take away my reproach among men.**"* (Luke 1:25)

Most casual Bible readers take this verse as a gracious word of thanksgiving to God, and nothing more. What they miss is Elizabeth's very *biblical* faith. For, in her gracious thanksgiving to God, she is also quoting Scripture. In specific, she is quoting Rachel, the wife of Jacob, who said the following after God granted her a miraculous pregnancy:

*She conceived, bore a son, and said, "**God has taken away my reproach.**"* (Gen 30:23)

Yet there is more. The Prophet Isaiah paints an exquisite Gospel picture for Israel whose subject is a barren woman who, one day, miraculously finds herself to be the mother of a great multitude of children. Elizabeth knew the Prophet's painting very well. Her gracious thanksgiving to God is a direct allusion to this ancient biblical text:

*"Sing, **O barren**, you who did not give birth; break out into singing, and cry aloud, you who did not travail with child: for more are the children of the desolate than the children of the married wife," says the* LORD....*"Do not be afraid; for you will not be ashamed. Do not be confounded; for you will not be disappointed. For you will forget the shame of your youth; and* **the reproach** *of your widowhood you shall remember no more."* (Isa 54:1, 4)

A second example of Elizabeth's deep knowledge of the Bible is found in her words to Mary. When Mary, her relative, comes to greet her, she pronounces a blessing over Mary:

*She called out with a loud voice, and said, "**Blessed are you among women**, and **blessed is the fruit of your womb!**"* (Luke 1:42)

Once again, these are not merely spontaneous, highly emotional words of jubilee. They are also God-fearing, thoughtful words, taken straight from the pages of Holy Writ. Firstly, the *"blessed are you among women"* part of Elizabeth's blessing, given to Mary, is a quotation from the book of Judges: *"Jael shall be **blessed above women**, the wife of Heber the Kenite; **blessed shall she be above women** in the tent"* (Judges 5:24).[8]

---

[8] It might be disturbing, at first, to think that Elizabeth has Judges 5:24 in mind when blessing Mary. For, the blessing of Judges 5:24 is pronounced upon Jael, the woman who ended the tyranny of Jabin king of Canaan by killing his commander, Sisera, with a tent peg and a hammer. However, Mary, by giving birth to Jesus, is, in fact, helping to bring about the end of a much greater tyranny, to wit, the tyranny of Satan, sin, and death. Also, just as Jael won the battle not on the battlefield of men, but in the domestic realm, *"in the tent,"* so too does Mary achieve such a wonderful victory in her own domestic realm, by carrying, giving birth to, and subsequently nurturing the boy Jesus.

Secondly, the latter part of Elizabeth's blessing pronounced over Mary is also a quotation from the Bible. It is, actually, quite "pregnant" with biblical quotations and allusions:

*She called out with a loud voice, and said, "Blessed are you among women, and **blessed is the fruit of your womb**!"* (Luke 1:42)

*Joseph is a fruitful vine, **a fruitful vine** by a spring. His branches run over the wall....the Almighty...will bless you, with blessings of heaven above, blessings of the deep that lies below, **blessings** of the breasts, and **of the womb**.* (Genesis 49:22, 25)

*Behold, children are a heritage of the LORD. **The fruit of the womb** is [a] reward.* (Psalm 127:3)

*The LORD has sworn to David in truth. He will not turn from it: "I will set **the fruit of your [womb]** on your throne."*[9] (Psalm 132:11)

John the Baptist, then, is *Elizabeth's* babe. For, where did John get his great knowledge of Holy Scripture? Where did he learn how to stand against the sins of the world, and be immovable? Who taught John how to suffer like a good soldier of Christ Jesus? Who helped John to see the centrality of the Messiah in the Old Testament? From what God-fearing source did John learn his great humility? Is not Elizabeth's motherhood (along with Zacharias' fatherhood), coupled with his being *"filled with the Holy Spirit, even from*

---

[9] Most English translations say, *"the fruit of your body,"* so as to make the metaphor match David's masculinity. But the Hebrew is strongly connected to the language of *"the fruit"* of the *"womb,"* which makes the Psalm 132:11–Luke 1:42 connection quite Messianic, indeed!

his mother's womb" (Luke 1:15), very much the source of all of these marvelous things?

Think, then, of how God used Elizabeth's God-centered (and very much *domestic*) motherhood to train her son, John. For, what would have happened if Elizabeth had been an ambitious career woman, and had cast Baby John into a daycare center when he was a mere six weeks old? What would have become of John if Elizabeth had been into cosmetics, jewelry, and trendy fashions, rather than modesty, submission, and the fear of God? What if Elizabeth had envisioned for her son a lucrative pharmaceutical career, rather than dedicating him to the sovereign will of God? What would have happened to this boy, this Elijah-who-was-to-come, had Elizabeth taught him a cheap, flow-with-the-culture "Gospel," rather than trained him to take a prophetic, no-compromise stand against the deeply depraved culture surrounding him?

The Church in the Western world needs to repent over the rampant devaluation of motherhood in her midst. For, in the face of modern feminism, an appalling number of pastors in the Church have proved themselves to be ashamed of the Gospel as it relates to the primarily domestic ministry of mothers in the life of the nuclear family (again, Titus 2:5). Many men in the Church have self-interestedly coaxed their wives into a "double income" mindset. Not a few women in the Church have selfishly valued money, career, and personal recreation over bountiful procreation and the sacrificial pains of distinctly Christian child rearing. Very few Christian mothers in today's Church follow God's plan and spoken decrees concerning the education of their children (Deuteronomy 6:1-9).[10] In sum, the ethos of the

---

[10] Yet there is, no doubt, a very faithful and persevering remnant of such mothers who do have a biblical understanding of the education/discipleship of children, as evidenced by the striking growth of the Christian home education movement during the last few decades.

modern Church has grossly twisted and distorted God's will for Christian motherhood. It is no wonder, then, that not many giant, Wesley-sized "voices calling in the wilderness" are forthcoming from the midst of her membership.

O beloved Christian Sisters, did not the Lord make you distinctly feminine, in fearful and wonderful fashion? Will you, then, love God enough to give the lie to the modern redefinitions of womanhood?

If so, are you faithfully imitating Elizabeth, in all of her exemplary piety? Do you know your Bible the way in which Elizabeth knew her Bible? Or do you make excuses for yourself so that you feel no need to reach to the heights that Elizabeth did in treasuring and memorizing the Scriptures? Are you yourself willing to suffer for the sake of righteousness? Are you, in turn, preparing your children to be ready to suffer for the sake of righteousness? Are you teaching your children to flow with the sins of culture, or else, perhaps, simply to ignore the sins of culture, or are you teaching them to speak out against the sins of culture, and to call people to repent of those sins, lest the ax of God fall upon the root of the tree? O Sister, beloved of God, be crucified to the modern "feminisms" of this world, and instead take up the fruitful (yet cross-bearing) labors of quiet, submissive, joyful, plentiful, nurturing, world-changing, *biblical* motherhood.

ELIZABETH'S BABE IS A "BABE" IN THE WOMB

We want to understand better the babe in Elizabeth's womb. In this desire, we have sought to understand better the babe's mother, Elizabeth. We have found her to be a righteous, wonderfully Word-centered mother. Next, let us observe that the babe in Elizabeth's womb is called a *"babe"* even in the womb!

*For behold, when the voice of your greeting came into my ears, the **baby** leaped in my womb for joy! (Luke 1:44)*

In 1534, William Tyndale (c. 1494-1536) translated the Greek word *bréphos* in this verse as *"babe,"* and he did so very judiciously. This is not a potential human, but an actual person. In Holy Scripture, there is no difference in *personhood* between preborn and post-born babies. For, the Greek word *bréphos* is used to describe both the preborn John the Baptist and the post-born Baby Jesus:

*This is the sign to you: you will find a **Baby** wrapped in strips of cloth, lying in a feeding trough. (Luke 2:12)*

*They came with haste, and found both Mary and Joseph, and the **Baby** was lying in the feeding trough. (Luke 2:16)*

The lucidity of Scripture on this point is divinely intentional. God has spelled out for us, in clear Greek letters, the personhood of the baby in the womb. The *bréphos* is a *"babe"* in Elizabeth's womb; the *bréphos* is a *"Babe"* swaddled and lying in a manger. The only thing that has changed is environment. One "babe" is living in the warm, cozy quarters of Elizabeth's womb. The other "Babe," having been born, is lying exposed and vulnerable in a feeding trough.

Not only this, but Doctor Luke also sees other *bréphē* (the plural of *bréphos*) as "babes" elsewhere in his writings of Holy Scripture:

*They were also bringing their **babies** to him, that he might touch them. But when the disciples saw it, they rebuked them. (Luke 18:15)*

*The same [Pharaoh, king of Egypt] took advantage of our race, and mistreated our fathers, and forced them to throw out their **babies**, so that they would not stay alive.* (Acts 7:19)

John is a *"babe"* in Elizabeth's womb. This means that he has as much personhood, dignity, and worth as any *"babe"* that is outside of the womb. Moreover, he is fully alive in the womb. For, John, the babe in Elizabeth's womb, *"leaps for joy"* on account of the other Babe—the Babe who is in Mary's womb:

*For behold, when the voice of your greeting came into my ears, the baby **leaped** in my womb **for joy**!* (Luke 1:44)

Only persons feel joy! So John's personhood in the womb is established. Moreover, Baby Jesus is in His first trimester in Mary's womb.[11] And it is the Personhood of Jesus that causes John to leap for joy in Elizabeth's womb. Therefore, the Personhood of Jesus in the womb is established, biblically, as early as the first trimester of pregnancy. This means that nursing infants do not have any more "personhood" than do babies in the womb. It also means that newly conceived babies do not have any less "personhood" than do third-trimester babies in the womb. All babies, from conception onwards, are fully alive, with full "personhood" in the womb.

Predictably, however, what Holy Scripture makes clear, Satan seeks to make ambiguous. He wants moral lines to be made quite fuzzy, and black-and-white matters to become

---

[11] The evidence for this is as follows. First, Luke 1:36 says that Elizabeth is in her *"sixth month"* of pregnancy when Mary, the virgin, miraculously conceives Baby Jesus. Second, John the Baptist is, obviously, still in Elizabeth's womb when Mary visits Elizabeth (Luke 1:44). Therefore, Mary's visit to Elizabeth must take place within three months of Baby Jesus' conception, for otherwise John the Baptist would have already been born.

THE BABES OF CHRISTMAS

gray. Satan works hard on pastors, using every compromised Bible commentary and every church-political pressure that is within his grasp to get them willfully to ignore the Abortion Abolitionism that God has woven into the first two chapters of the Gospel of Luke. He also coerces physicians, lawyers, professors, and politicians—strong-arming them with phrases such as "academic protocol" and "proper medical and legal terminology"—into using the ambiguous Latin term *fetus* in place of the more definitive English term "baby." In all of these crafty and wily ways, the truth is not contradicted, but simply smeared, and, therefore, cast into doubt.

Yet God's Word remains plain and perspicuous in the hearts of those who fear Him. You, O Christian, know the truth. You know that the child is a full *bréphos*, a full *"baby"* in the womb. You care for these precious little human beings who are being murdered, day after day, in cities and towns across the globe. Since you love Jesus Christ, you weep and weep over this silent Holocaust in our world. Therefore, you count it a privilege to be on Christian pilgrimage with fellow believers who are risking life and limb in order to protect children in the womb; and you yourself would count it a privilege to suffer persecution for the sake of the defense of the preborn person in the womb. This is why, dear Christian, you are reading this book, and this is why the present author has much hope that God's Abolitionist work shall yet be fulfilled, some magnificent day.

ELIZABETH'S BABE IS A JOYFUL BABE

In order to understand Elizabeth's babe, we must first understand his mother. He is, after all, *Elizabeth's* babe. Yes, and in order to understand her *babe*, we must believe that he is, in fact, a full babe, a full person in Elizabeth's womb. He is not a blob of tissue. Rather, from conception onwards, he is a person, created in the image of God.

Still, there is one remaining observation about Elizabeth's babe that is vital to our understanding of the Gospel. It is that he, John the Baptist, is a *joyful* babe:

*For behold, when the voice of your greeting came into my ears, the baby **leaped in my womb for joy**!* (Luke 1:44)

The Gospel is joyful. For Doctor Luke, the whole Christmas account is soaked with joy:

*You will have **joy** and gladness; and many will **rejoice** at his birth.* (Luke 1:14)

*My spirit has **rejoiced** in God my Savior.* (Luke 1:47)

*The angel said to them, "Do not be afraid, for behold, I bring you good news of **great joy** which will be to all the people."* (Luke 2:10)

Why is this? Why is John such a joyful babe in Elizabeth's womb? John's joy announces the coming of Immanuel, for John's whole life is lived as the herald of the coming Immanuel. For, John the Baptist is:

The voice of one who calls out, *"Prepare the way of the* LORD *in the wilderness! Make a level highway in the desert for our God."* (Isaiah 40:3)

He is, if the disciples of Jesus are willing to receive it, the Elijah who was to come:

*Behold, **I will send you Elijah the prophet** before the great and terrible day of the* LORD *comes.* (Malachi 4:5)

Why, then, is John so joyful? He is joyful because He has seen the Lord's Anointed. In Elizabeth's womb, he senses the

nearness of the Lord when Mary draws near to greet
Elizabeth. When he is grown into adulthood, he beholds the
Lamb of God who takes away the sins of the world. He sees
Him, and recognizes Him, for the Spirit of God descends
upon Him as a dove, and remains on Him. The servant
joyfully announces the arrival of the Master. The best man at
the wedding joyfully heralds the arrival of the Bridegroom:

> He who has the bride is the bridegroom; but the friend of the
> bridegroom, who stands and hears him, **rejoices greatly**
> because of the bridegroom's voice. This, **my joy**, therefore is
> made full. (John 3:29)

The joy of John the Baptist is the joy of the Gospel. John
is the herald of that joy. The Gospel is so brilliant in its act of
setting men free from the everlasting consequences of sin
and death that it causes men to *"leap"* for *"joy,"* just as the
babe, John, *"leaped"* for *"joy"* in Elizabeth's womb:

> Then the lame man **will leap** like a deer, and the tongue of the
> mute will sing; for waters will break out in the wilderness, and
> streams in the desert....The LORD's ransomed ones will return,
> and come with singing to Zion; and **everlasting joy** will be on
> their heads. They will obtain **gladness and joy**, and sorrow
> and sighing will flee away. (Isaiah 35:6, 10)

Why is the babe in Elizabeth's womb a leaping babe?
Why is he such a joyful babe? The precious, tiny, preborn
Lamb of God is in Mary's womb. John, in Elizabeth's womb,
senses the close proximity of the Lamb of God in Mary's
womb. Thus the proximity of the Lamb of God causes John
to have so much joy that he must leap in his own mother's
womb!

Yet who is this Lamb of God? He is *"the Lamb of God, who
takes away the sin of the world"* (John 1:29). He is not only
Mary's *"firstborn"* (Matthew 1:25), born of a woman, but also

God's own *"Firstborn"* (Hebrews 1:6), born of God, who is sacrificed in order to make appeasement for the sins of all men. In Abraham's day, Isaac was spared. Abraham's firstborn was spared the knife. Yet God the Father does not spare His Firstborn. He allows the knife to be lowered on Jesus—for that is how dark and horrible our sin really is! The horror of human sin against God is displayed in the horror of the slaughter of God's Firstborn on the cross.

Yet the joy of the Gospel is that the Lamb of God is also the Lion of Judah. He, *"the Lion who is of the tribe of Judah, the Root of David, has overcome, He who opens the book and its seven seals"* (Revelation 5:5). Thus as Lamb, He dies; yet as Lion, He rises, rules, and judges. The Firstborn, slaughtered, has become the Firstborn, raised from the grave, exalted to the right hand of the Father, and ruling over the kings of the earth. He, God's Firstborn, shall reign upon His Father's throne, forever and ever!

To see Jesus is to see God (John 14:9). Certainly, the triune God, who is one in essence, exists, eternally, as three distinct Persons. Still, to see Jesus is to look upon God's glory revealed in the human face of God's Firstborn (2 Corinthians 4:6). This is why Jesus says:

> *"Your father Abraham **rejoiced** to see My day. He **saw** it, and **was glad**."* (John 8:56)

The Gospel is the astonishing joy of Immanuel, "God with us." It is God having come near to us in human flesh. It is also the coming glory of Christ Jesus that is yet to be revealed. For, the Son of Man came, in Mary's womb, in infinite meekness. Yet He shall return on the clouds, with the holy angels, in infinite glory. This is the permanent, Gospel joy that not even intense sufferings and persecutions can snatch from our hearts:

*But rejoice because you are partakers of Christ's sufferings, that at the revelation of His glory you also may rejoice **with exceeding joy**.* (1 Peter 4:13)

John, the joyful babe, heralds the glad tidings of a joyful eternity with God, for those who fear Him. He joyfully announces the coming of the Lamb of God into the world, and his Gospel proclamation starts even in the womb. He is an evangelist even in Elizabeth's womb! He evades the praise of men, that Christ may have His proper glory. John humbly decreases, that Christ might increase. He points his disciples not to himself, and his baptism—which is by water—but rather to the Lamb of God, and His baptism—which is by the Holy Spirit and by fire. In doing so, he teaches one of his disciples, who is another "John," how to rejoice in the Gospel of the Lamb. For it is John, the Apostle, who tells us of ineffable joy of the wedding feast of the Lamb:

*Let us [be glad] **and [rejoice]**, and let us give the glory to Him! For **the marriage of the Lamb** has come, and His wife has made herself ready.* (Revelation 19:7)

Christmas, then, is a time to remember John the Baptist, the joyful babe. Yet the brilliance of John's humility is seen in the fact that as soon as we remember him at Christmas time, we immediately find our gaze riveted upon the Person of Jesus. The leaping babe exists only to herald the divine Babe. The sole intention of the son of Elizabeth is to give maximum glory to the Son of Mary. This is John's joyful calling, and he does, indeed, remain faithful to it all his life, even up to and through his humble martyrdom. Great, then, is John's reward in the Kingdom of Heaven.

Dear Reader, what is your source of joy at Christmas time? Do you find yourself, in this parched world, thirsting for joy, and yet trying to quench your thirst by drinking from broken cisterns that can hold no water? Do you know how to come to the fountain of living waters, and how to drink from that fountain at Christmas time? Is the radiant, eternal glory of Christ Jesus—a radiant, eternal glory that condescended to reside in Mary's womb—the center of your Christmas, and thus the fountainhead of your joy?

If so, then let the world see your joy. Celebrate Christmas with the unveiled face of a man or woman who has beheld the light of the knowledge of the glory of God in the face of Jesus Christ. Let the wonder of Christmas cause your own heart to leap for joy, and let the light of the Gospel of the glory of Christ illuminate your own face. Then, when others ask you whence you draw such living waters of undiminishing joy, you can say to them, with holy glee, "Oh, if you would really like to know, the off-road, narrow path to the fountainhead of my joy begins with a marvelous, historical account. That account starts with a barren woman named Elizabeth, and it involves a most joyful babe, who once leaped for joy in his mother's womb." Amen.

5

THE DAVIDIC BABE:
Jesus' Messianic Blessing and Preborn Children

(Matthew 1:1-17)

*The book of the genealogy of Jesus Christ, the Son of **David**, the Son of Abraham. Abraham became the father of Isaac. Isaac became the father of Jacob. Jacob became the father of Judah and his brothers. Judah became the father of Perez and Zerah by Tamar. Perez became the father of Hezron. Hezron became the father of Ram. Ram became the father of Amminadab. Amminadab became the father of Nahshon. Nahshon became the father of Salmon. Salmon became the father of Boaz by Rahab. Boaz became the father of Obed by Ruth. Obed became the father of Jesse. Jesse became the father of King **David**. **David** became the father of Solomon by her who had been Uriah's wife. Solomon became the father of Rehoboam. Rehoboam became the father of Abijah. Abijah became the father of Asa. Asa became the father of Jehoshaphat. Jehoshaphat became the father of Joram. Joram became the father of Uzziah. Uzziah became the father of Jotham. Jotham became the father of Ahaz. Ahaz became the father of Hezekiah. Hezekiah became the father of Manasseh. Manasseh became the father of Amon. Amon became the father of Josiah. Josiah became the father of Jechoniah and his brothers, at the time of the exile to Babylon. After the exile to Babylon, Jechoniah became the father of Shealtiel. Shealtiel became the father of Zerubbabel. Zerubbabel became the father of Abiud. Abiud became the father of Eliakim. Eliakim became the father of Azor. Azor became the father of Zadok. Zadok became the father of Achim. Achim became the father of Eliud. Eliud became the father of Eleazar. Eleazar became the father of Matthan. Matthan became the father of Jacob. Jacob became the father of Joseph, the husband of Mary, from whom was born Jesus, who is called Christ. So all the generations from Abraham to **David** are fourteen generations; from **David** to the exile to Babylon fourteen generations; and from the carrying away to Babylon to the Christ, fourteen generations.*
(Matthew 1:1-17)

GOD is Lord over history. He has ordered the history of Israel around the throne of His servant, David. In this genealogy of Jesus, which constitutes the opening words of the New Testament Scriptures, we see that the Holy Spirit has inspired Matthew, the Apostle, to write with King David in mind. For, the entire genealogy is structured around David:

*So all the generations from Abraham **to David** are fourteen generations; **from David** to the exile to Babylon fourteen generations; and from the carrying away to Babylon **to the Christ** [i.e. the Son of David], fourteen generations.* (Matthew 1:17)

Noticeably, the number *"fourteen"* is very important in Matthew's genealogy. Matthew very purposefully has omitted four generations in the middle section of the genealogy (those of Ahaziah, Joash, Amaziah, and Jehoiakim).[1] He has done this so as to create a triad of "fourteen's" in the genealogy:

*So all the generations from Abraham to David are **fourteen generations**; from David to the exile to Babylon **fourteen***

---

[1] Matthew omits the three immediate descendants of evil Queen Athaliah: (i) Ahaziah, the wicked son of Athaliah (2 Chronicles 22:2-3); (ii) Ahaziah's son, Joash, who apostatized from the faith towards the end of his life (2 Chronicles 24:17-22); and (iii) Joash's son, Amaziah, who also apostatized (2 Chronicles 25:27). All three of these men, Ahaziah, Joash, and Amaziah, died the ignoble death of being murdered by their own countrymen. Thus the sons of evil Queen Athaliah are omitted from the genealogy "to the third generation" (cf. Exodus 34:6). Matthew also omits Jehoiakim, perhaps on account of his extreme wickedness, even to the point of being blasphemous enough to burn the scroll of the Prophet Jeremiah, thus prompting the Lord's curse upon him: *"Therefore the LORD says concerning Jehoiakim king of Judah: **He will have no one to sit on David's throne**; and his dead body shall be cast out in the day to the heat, and in the night to the frost"* (Jeremiah 36:30).

*generations; and from the carrying away to Babylon to the Christ, **fourteen generations**.* (Matthew 1:17)

Why *"fourteen"*? Why does the Apostle want us to see *"fourteen"* generations from Abraham to the rise of the Davidic monarchy, another *"fourteen"* generations during the reign of the Davidic monarchy, and then *"fourteen"* more generations from the fall of the Davidic monarchy until the coming of the Christ, the Son of David? It is hard to be certain, but it is at least possible that Matthew, as a thoroughly Jewish thinker, pays special attention to the numerical value of David's name. His Hebrew name, *d-w-d* (that is, "David" without the vowels, and with the Hebrew *"w"* representing our English *"v"*), carries a numerical value of *"fourteen."*[2]

If this is Matthew's reason for structuring Jesus' genealogy into three sets of *"fourteen,"* then David is, indeed, the central figure in the genealogy. More specifically, David is the central "type" of Christ in the genealogy, and David's role as a Messianic "type" is to prepare the way for one of his own descendants, the Son of David, to far surpass him in kingship and glory. David is Israel's great king, but the Son of David shall be David's Lord (Psalm 110:1).

During the time of Jesus' birth, Israel's only hope is in the restoration of David's throne. Suffering under the brutality of Roman rule, much like her suffering in Egypt

---

[2] The Hebrew *"d"* is the fourth letter of the Hebrew alphabet, giving it a numerical value of **4**. The Hebrew *"w"* is the sixth letter of the Hebrew alphabet, giving it a numerical value of **6**. The numerical value of David's name, then, is easily calculated as *"d+w+d"* or **4+6+4 = 14**. This is something that Jewish readers would quickly pick up on, as they were quite used to associating important names with their respective numeric values (thus Robert H. Gundry, *Matthew: A Commentary on His Handbook for a Mixed Church under Persecution* [2nd ed.; Grand Rapids: W.B. Eerdmans, 1994], 19 — though the present author strongly rejects Gundry's general, higher-critical approach to the Gospel of Matthew).

during the years leading up to the Exodus, with bloodshed, persecution, and oppression encompassing her daily, her hope is fixed solely upon a new, revived Davidic monarchy. Languishing under her cruel bondage to Rome, Israel groans and cries to God for the fallen tabernacle of David to be restored:

> *In that day I will raise up **the tent of David** who is fallen, and close up its breaches, and I will raise up its ruins, and I will build it as in the days of old.* (Amos 9:11)

Christmas, then, is about the birth of the Son of David. It is about the rebirth of the Davidic monarchy, yet in a truly transcendent and Heavenly way. At Christmas, the throne of David is restored to Israel. On Christmas Day, the highest and greatest King of all of human history is born.[3]

Yet how can this be? If Israel's Messiah, the King of kings, is born on Christmas Day, then why are the conditions of His royal birth so rude and unbecoming of royalty? Where are the soft, purple receiving blankets for the Baby? Where are the royal nurses? Why are the royal trumpets of Rome not sounding at Jesus' birth, and why are the priestly Temple choirs of Israel not singing to laud His arrival?

If this is truly the Son of David, then clearly both Rome and Israel are not prepared to acknowledge Him as such. He is born in obscurity. At the Manger, there are only donkeys braying, lowly shepherds inquiring, and swaddling clothes wrapping the cold, shivering Babe who is lying in an animal stall. He, the Son of David, is despised and rejected by men, a Babe of sorrows, and familiar with sickness and suffering.

---

[3] Christmas Day, of course, is not the actual calendar day of Christ's birth, which is unknown. It is, rather, a memorial celebration of the day on which Christ was born.

Yet this, too, fits the title *"the Son of David."* For David, himself, started out as a lowly shepherd. He spent many nights outside in the cold, caring for his little lambs. He, too, was more welcomed by the animals than by his own brothers.

JESUS CHRIST, THE SON OF DAVID

*"The book of the genealogy of Jesus Christ, **the Son of David**...."* (Matthew 1:1)

Who, then, is the Son of David? In Holy Scripture, all of the *"Son of David"* prophecies are rooted in God's Word to King David through the prophet Nathan:

*When your days are fulfilled, and you sleep with your fathers, I will set up your offspring after you, **who will proceed out of your body**, and **I will establish his kingdom**. He will build a house for My name, and **I will establish the throne of his kingdom forever**.* (2 Samuel 11:12-13)

Solomon, the son of David, built a house for the Lord's name. However, Solomon himself is not the final fulfillment of this prophecy. For, the prophecy establishes the great "Davidic hope" that a descendent of David would arise and establish not a temporary, but an everlasting throne in Israel:

*I have made a covenant with My chosen one, I have sworn to David, My servant, "I will establish your offspring **forever**, and build up your throne **to all generations**."* (Psalm 89:3–4)

This is God's promise to David, known in Christian theology as the "Davidic Covenant." The covenant is a conditional one for David's human descendants. That is, its blessing of kingship and a perpetual dynasty is conditional upon obedience to God's covenantal laws and testimonies:

*For Your servant David's sake, do not turn away the face of Your anointed one. The LORD has sworn to David in truth. He will not turn from it: "I will set the fruit of your body on your throne. **If your children will keep My covenant, My testimony that I will teach them**, their children also will sit on your throne forever more."* (Psalm 132:10-12)

Sadly, of course, David's descendants did not keep God's holy covenantal laws. King Ahaz practiced child sacrifice *"according to the abominations of the nations whom the LORD cast out from before the children of Israel,"* and he sacrificed and burned incense on the high places, even under every green tree (2 Kings 16:3-4). King Manasseh *"built altars for all the host of the heavens in the two courts of the LORD's house,"* and he employed divination, witchcraft, and the work of spiritists in his governing affairs. He even put a carved image of the goddess Asherah in the Temple of the Lord (2 Kings 21:5-6). Jehoichin (called *"Jeconiah"* both in 1 Chronicles 3:16 and in Matthew's genealogy), the man who took the title of Davidic kingship with him into exile in Babylon, *"did that which was evil in the LORD's sight, according to all that his father had done"* (2 Kings 24:9).

As a result of all of this spiritual apostasy, the Davidic monarchy was shattered. Upon invading Jerusalem at the beginning of the sixth century BC, the Babylonians not only destroyed the Temple in Jerusalem, but also crushed the Davidic dynasty in Jerusalem. Therefore, the Jews clung to the promises of the great Prophets of Israel, in hopes that a "new David" would someday arise:

*Of the increase of His government and of peace there shall be no end, **on David's throne, and on his kingdom**, to establish it, and to uphold it with justice and with righteousness from that time on, **even forever**. The zeal of the LORD of Hosts will perform this.* (Isaiah 9:7)

It was, after all, the Prophets who foresaw the reestablishment of the Davidic monarchy coming about only through God's special Servant, His Messiah. It was to be the Christ, and Him alone, who would come to restore David's fallen tent:

My Servant David [that is, the Son of David] *shall be **King** over them; and they all shall have **one Shepherd**: they shall also walk in My ordinances, and observe My statutes, and do them.* (Ezekiel 37:24)

Also,

*Afterward the children of Israel shall return, and seek the LORD their God, **and David their King** [again, the Son of David], and shall come with trembling to the LORD and to His blessings in the last days.* (Hosea 3:5)

What, then, does this mean for Christmas? It means that the weak, vulnerable Baby in the manger is really a mighty, powerful King. He is the heir to the throne of David. He is the One who shall reign upon David's throne forever and ever:

*He will be great, and will be called the Son of the Most High. The Lord God will give Him **the throne of His father, David**.* (Luke 1:32)

This, in turn, means that the Babe in the manger has both a Davidic glory and a Heavenly glory. Prior to His resurrection from the dead, He has no form, nor majesty that we should take note of Him. Yet after His resurrection, His Davidic glory — namely, that He is the true Son of David — is revealed to the world:

*Remember Jesus Christ, **risen from the dead, of the offspring of David**, according to my gospel....* (2 Timothy 2:8)

Yet Jesus' Davidic glory is unique, for His Person is uniquely divine. Not only that, but He saves His people not through the conquest of the sword (as with King David), but rather through the offering of His own blood for the forgiveness of sins (He conquers by His own blood). Therefore, He alone is worthy to open the Heavenly scroll and its seven seals. And thus His Davidic glory also reveals a Heavenly glory:

> *One of the elders said to me, "Do not weep. Behold, the Lion who is of the tribe of Judah, **the Root of David**, has overcome; He who opens the book and its seven seals." ...They sang a new song, saying, "**You are worthy** to take the book, and to open its seals: for **You were [slain]**, and [redeemed] us for God **with Your blood**, out of every tribe, language, people, and nation."* (Revelation 5:5, 9)

How, then, does the Lord Jesus establish His everlasting throne? He, the Son of David conquers, both spiritually and politically, *by His own blood*. King David was mighty with the sword. However, with the historical arrival of the Babe in the manger, One mightier than David has come. Yet this Babe, this Son of David who is so mighty, grows up to prove His might not on the battlefield, but on the cross. He conquers the world, in love, by offering His own blood as the appeasing sacrifice[4] for the sins of the whole world (1 John 2:2).

---

[4] Christ's blood is an "appeasing sacrifice" in that God's wrath must be poured out in response to the horrific nature of human sin. The atonement of Christ's blood, however, is *not* universally applied to all men—as if all men shall be saved. For, there are vast multitudes of men who, through their unbelief, reject Jesus' atoning blood. Thus instead of having the wrath of God "appeased" on their behalf at the cross of

William Tyndale, who translated the Bible into English at a time when doing so was a capital crime, was for many years a Protestant fugitive in Europe, being pursued by the agents of the Roman Catholic zealot Sir Thomas More. During most of the cat and mouse game between More and Tyndale, it was More who was Chancellor of England and who had the political approval of King Henry VIII to pursue Tyndale's capture and execution as a "heretic." Thus More was politically mighty, while Tyndale was a mere nuisance in the eyes of the Crown.

Yet the publication of Tyndale's *The Obedience of a Christian Man* had won him a certain amount of respect in the eyes of King Henry,[5] and More's refusal to support the king's lusty desire to divorce Catherine of Aragon in order to marry Anne Boleyn had put More under the king's ire. It would have been quite expedient, then, for Tyndale to write to the king, as a Protestant (for Anne Boleyn had Protestant sympathies, after all), in support of the king's desire for a divorce, and thus sympathize with the king over the Pope's tyrannical jurisdiction over England (for the Pope was not at all eager to cooperate with Henry on annulling his marriage to Catherine). Had Tyndale done so, he might reasonably have expected a speedy pardon from the king.

However, Tyndale was a man of conviction, not of political maneuvering. He wrote against the idea of a marriage annulment with Catherine, and said that Scripture would not permit it. He called the king to repent, and to fear God, lest God's anger bring about the destruction of the king's realm.[6] This evoked the king's wrath against Tyndale, which in turn prevented Tyndale's return to England and

Christ, they shall, upon their death, face the unmitigated, everlasting wrath of God that is poured out upon them in response to their sins.
[5] For the historical details of this, see Brian Moynahan, *God's Bestseller: William Tyndale, Thomas More, and the Writing of the English Bible – A Story of Martyrdom and Betrayal* (New York: St. Martin's Press, 2002), 161.
[6] Ibid., 221.

kept him on the Continent. It was there, on the Continent, that Tyndale eventually was betrayed, caught, and martyred—being strangled first, and subsequently being burned at the stake.

O how many juggling compromisers in today's Church would want to chastise Tyndale for his moral scrupulousness! They would want to say to him, "William, you could have won the political war against Catholicism and Popery by siding with the king! All you had to do was admit the need for annulment. And the marriage was already shot through with holes—it was already a done deal. O foolish William, why be such a moralist, especially when you could have won the political war for Protestantism!"

Yet the truth of the matter is that Tyndale did win the political war against Catholicism and Popery. However, he won it the way in which his Master had won the world. He followed the Son of David in conquering not by sword, but by blood. Tyndale conquered by being a true disciple and subject of the Son of David.

Matthew's genealogy tells us that Jesus Christ, the Son of David, came to earth to conquer the earth. His is, in fact, a truly political (even as it is also truly spiritual and Heavenly) conquest. Yet His conquest is not one that He has obtained through sword and shield, or bow and arrow. Rather, He has conquered by way of His own blood. This is what gives Him the divine right to sit, everlastingly, upon the throne of His ancestor, David.

There is a political war raging in the Western world today. It is a war against babies, wherein both doctors and parents fight for their supposed "right" to murder babies, and already torrents of innocent blood have been shed in this war. It is also a war against Christianity. It is being fought with much bigotry against Christians. In this war, those who hate the teachings of historic Christianity are issuing to us who love those sacred teachings a highly political, "Change, or die!" ultimatum.

Following our King, the Son of David, we must fight and conquer the very way in which He fought and conquered. Therefore, our motto must not be, "We are here to win souls, not fight political wars," for the Kingdom of the Son of David is very much a political one, and not only a spiritual one (it comes *"on earth, as it is in Heaven"*). Nor can our motto be, "Let us work hard to elect the right president, senators, and congressmen who will win the war for us," since almost all such "candidates" (with a very few bright exceptions) have proved themselves to be unwilling to pay the price of true Christian discipleship[7] that it costs to win the war. Lastly, we must certainly not — may it never be! — say with the compromisers, "We need to make political concessions regarding our biblical convictions in order to obtain the desired goal of winning the war."

Instead, our job is to fight the way in which Tyndale did. We must be willing to suffer for the truth. Then, as we suffer for the truth, we must set our gaze on the Son of David and await the justice of His coming Kingdom. When we are losing and dying, we must remember that we are actually winning and conquering. Loving our enemies, and blessing them when they curse us, we shall win the war. Filling up in our flesh what is lacking in His afflictions (in His body, the Church), we shall conquer with Him. And when the sufferings and persecutions are at their worst, we shall cry out, in faith and boldness, "The Son of David shall come! He shall come and sit upon the throne of David! The Son of David shall come and bring justice and righteousness upon the earth!"

---

[7] This "price of true Christian discipleship" may be summarized as follows: *"Greater love has no one than this, that someone lay down his life for his friends"* (John 15:13), and also, *"By this we know love, because He laid down His life for us. And we ought to lay down our lives for the brothers"* (1 John 3:16).

113

THE SON OF DAVID IS ALSO THE SON OF ABRAHAM

Matthew's genealogy is vast and rich! The Son of Mary is the Son of David. He is the One who shall sit upon the throne of His father, David, forever and ever. Yet, there is even more. The Son of Mary is also *the Son of Abraham*:

The book of the genealogy of Jesus Christ, the Son of David, **the Son of Abraham**. *Abraham became the father of Isaac. Isaac became the father of Jacob. Jacob became the father of Judah and his brothers.* (Matthew 1:1-2)

Doctor Luke, the Apostle Paul's companion, emphasizes in his Gospel the descent of Jesus from Adam. Jesus is, indeed, *"the Son of Adam"* (Luke 3:38). However, the Apostle Matthew's emphasis is different. It is less ontological (that is, less focused on the essence of Jesus' human nature, as joined with his divine nature), and more covenantal. Like Luke, Matthew knows Jesus as *"the Son of Adam,"* to be sure, but the Holy Spirit has inspired Matthew to speak more to the covenantal nature of Jesus' genealogy. Jesus of Nazareth is the true, covenantal Son. He is the *"Son of Abraham"* who fulfills, in His own Person, the covenant that God made with Abraham:

I will make of you [Abraham] a great nation. I will bless you and make your name great. You will be a blessing. I will bless those who bless you, and I will curse him who curses you. ***All the families of the earth will be blessed through you.*** (Genesis 12:2–3)

Is Abraham's blessing for the Jews only? No, it is also for the Gentiles. For, it is not the sons of the flesh who inherit the blessing, but the sons of the promise. Also, the covenant states, *"All the families of the earth will be blessed through you"* (v. 3). Therefore, the fulfillment of the Abrahamic Covenant must come in such a way that both Jews and Gentiles (of all tongues, tribes, and nations) are recipients of this great blessing from God.

Why, then, are there women in Jesus' genealogy? If the Apostle Matthew's patriarchal retelling of the genealogy of Jesus is interrupted four times by the inclusion of women's names, what is God's purpose in doing this? Is the New Covenant a feminist one, and this is our first New Testament hint at that? Should Galatians 3:28, *"There is **neither Jew nor Greek**, there is neither slave nor free man, there is **neither male nor female**; for you are all one in Christ Jesus,"* be reinterpreted in hyper-Protestant, anti-historic-Christian fashion[8] to extend the blessings of the Abrahamic Covenant to women pastors and homosexual marriages? Is the multi-ethnic inclusivism of the Abrahamic Covenant to be extended (far beyond its original, Scriptural borders) to be an inclusivism that also embraces husband and wife role reversals in the home and "Christians" in the Church with "homosexual identities"? May it never be! For, feminism is seen as a heretical ideology in the Apostolic commandments of the New Covenant (see, for example, 1 Corinthians 11:3, 13-16; 1 Timothy 2:11-15), and homosexuality in the New Covenant remains what it was in the Old Covenant: a perverse and profane mentality, distorting the image of God in man at its deepest levels, and also an abominable sin (Leviticus 18:22; 20:13; Deuteronomy 22:5; Romans 1:26-27; 1 Corinthians 6:9-10).

Nevertheless, there are, indeed, four women included in the Apostle Matthew's genealogy of Jesus:

---

[8] The phrase "anti-historic-Christian" here means blatantly defying the interpretation of the Scriptures that has been normative throughout church history. In specific, none of the Church Fathers, Medieval theologians, Protestant Reformers, or Puritans would have allowed for this kind of feminist and/or homosexual reinterpretation of the Apostle Paul's words in Galatians 3:28.

*Judah became the father of Perez and Zerah **by Tamar**.... Salmon became the father of Boaz **by Rahab**. Boaz became the father of Obed **by Ruth**. Obed became the father of Jesse. Jesse became the father of King David. David became the father of Solomon **by her who had been Uriah's wife**.*
(Matthew 1:3, 5–6)

Why are these four women, Tamar, Rahab, Ruth, and Bathsheba, included in the genealogy? Is it because they all have scandalous pasts? Is this to show that Jesus came to save sinners, even women prostitutes and women caught in adultery (cf. John 8:3)? This is somewhat understandable guesswork, for this would fit the cases of Tamar, Rahab, and Bathsheeba. However, Ruth is never portrayed in God's Word in this light. She is, rather, always seen as pious, upright, and godly.[9]

We look elsewhere, then, for an explanation as to why the Spirit of God included Tamar, Rahab, Ruth, and Bathsheba in the Apostle Matthew's genealogy of Jesus. Yet we need not look far, for the answer lies right in the Apostle's text:

*The book of the genealogy of Jesus Christ, the Son of David, **the Son of Abraham**.* (Matthew 1:1)

Jesus Christ is not merely the Son of David, but also the Son of Abraham. As the Son of Abraham, He fulfills the Abrahamic Covenant in His very Person. Part of this includes Jesus Christ as being a blessing to *"all the families of the earth"* (again, Genesis 12:3). That is, the blessings of Jesus Christ extend beyond the Jews to all of the Gentiles of the world. Therefore, the most likely reason why Tamar, Rahab, Ruth, and Bathsheba are included in this genealogy is not

---

[9] Ruth 3:7-9 is not to be taken in any immodest manner, for both Boaz and Ruth were God-fearing in their persons and actions.

only that they are women (for the Gospel is for both men and women, to be sure!), but also that they are *Gentile* women. For, all four women are, most likely, Gentiles.

Jesus Christ, the Son of David, is also the Son of Abraham. Therefore, His blessings extend far beyond the realm of the Jews. They reach the Gentiles, even to the very ends of the earth:

> Let **the peoples** praise You, God. Let **all the peoples** praise You. The earth has yielded its increase. God, even our own God, will bless us. God will bless us. **All the ends of the earth shall fear Him**. (Psalm 67:5-7)

Israel is God's "*servant.*" As the servant of God, Israel is the means by which God fulfills His covenant with Abraham:

> But you, Israel, **My servant**, Jacob whom I have chosen, **the offspring of Abraham** My friend…. (Isaiah 41:8)

Yet as God's "*servant,*" Israel's fulfilling of the Abrahamic Covenant must include her role as a blessing to the Gentiles. She exists, in God's global plan, to be a "*light*" to the Gentiles:

> I, the LORD, have called you in righteousness, and will hold your hand, and will keep you, and make you **a covenant for the people, as a light for the nations**…. (Isaiah 42:6)

The Son of Mary, then, is not only the Son of David. He is also the Son of Abraham, which makes Him, in His very Person, a blessing to the Gentiles — that is, those Gentiles who shall hear the Gospel, repent and believe the Gospel, and come to worship at Mount Zion from the north and the south, and from the east and from the west:

*When Jesus heard it, He marveled, and said to those who followed, "Most certainly I tell you, I have not found so great a faith, not even in Israel. I tell you that **many will come from the east and the west**, and will sit down **with Abraham, Isaac, and Jacob in the Kingdom of Heaven….**"*
(Matthew 8:10–11)

The Son of Abraham comes to fulfill God's promise to Abraham, but Abraham, the Father of Faith, is not a father only to believing Jews. He also has many, many Gentile children who are his children by way of the promise:

*But it is not as though the Word of God has come to nothing. For they are not all Israel, that are of Israel. Neither, because they are Abraham's offspring, are they all children. But, "your offspring will be accounted as from Isaac." That is, it is not the children of the flesh who are children of God, **but the children of the promise are counted as heirs**.* (Romans 9:6–8)

Also,

*So then, **those who are of faith are blessed with the faithful Abraham**.* (Galatians 3:9)

And,

*[Christ took the curse in our stead]…**that the blessing of Abraham might come on the Gentiles through Christ Jesus**; that we might receive the promise of the Spirit through faith….If you are **Christ's**, then **you are Abraham's offspring** and heirs according to promise.* (Galatians 3:14, 29)

Jesus, as the Son of Abraham, grants even us, the once despised Gentiles, royal status in His Heavenly Kingdom! Therefore know, precious Reader, that the Son of Abraham has the divine power to transform your own genealogy.

Rahab may have looked in the mirror and said in her own mind, at one point in her life, "I am a wretched Canaanite. I am a filthy prostitute." Yet Rahab repented, turning away from the kingdom of Satan and towards the Kingdom of Light, and thus believed the promises of the God of Israel. Therefore, God now says to her, "You, Rahab, are an ancestor of Jesus, the Son of Abraham."

And you, precious Reader, may say in your mind, "I am the son of an alcoholic father and a thrice-married mother, and I myself have committed wretched sins against God. When I was younger, I even coaxed my girlfriend into having an abortion." Yet if you have been born again of the Spirit of life, having been washed in the blood of the Lamb and having learned, by faith, how to turn your back on the wicked ways of the world, and how to grow in your hatred of sin and in your love for the good and holy commandments of Christ, the Lord now says to you, "My child, you are born anew in the Gospel, and you are now called to be a faithful Christian husband, a godly Christian father, and a bold defender of life in the womb."

Moreover, since Jesus is not only the Son of David but also the Son of Abraham, the call of global evangelization is to be near the center of the life of the Church. On Christmas Day, the Church participates neither in the mythical idolatries of Santa Clause, nor the selfish indulgence of modern greed and materialism. Rather, on Christmas Day, the Church prays for the evangelization of lost souls in Morocco, Myanmar, and Bhutan, and for the courageous missionaries who are evangelizing them. Also, on Christmas Day, Christian parents gather their children and teach them the Scriptures concerning the Son of Abraham, thus training their children to preach Christ boldly to the lost, even being willing to give what they cannot keep in order to gain that which they cannot lose.[10]

JESUS CHRIST, THE SON OF GOD

The Apostle Matthew's genealogy of Jesus is much like George Frideric Handel's masterful oratorio, the *Messiah*. Like the *Messiah*, the genealogy carries the hearer through the vast, rich epochs of Holy Scripture in sweeping, sublime, and transcendent fashion.[11] And like the *Messiah*, the genealogy has a climactic, Heaven-infused "Hallelujah" chorus near its completion. For, the Son of Mary, who is the Son of David, who is the Son of Abraham, is, most importantly, *the very Son of God*:[12]

> *Jacob became the father of Joseph, the husband of **Mary, from whom** was born **Jesus**, who is called Christ.* (Matthew 1:16)

This is an astonishing verse, for in it there is a break in the human patriarchy of the genealogy. In the genealogy, Matthan became the father of Jacob, and Jacob became the

---

[10] We do, indeed, want to set Jim Elliot (1927-1956) before our children, at Christmas time, as a tremendous Christian role model.

[11] Of course, to the untrained ear, a mere Scriptural genealogy does not sound nearly as complex, nor as beautiful as a masterful oratorio. However, once the "theological music" of the genealogy is played in the human heart, by means of the Holy Spirit, it turns out to be breathtakingly beautiful.

[12] Some contemporary biblical scholars have tried to argue that Jesus' title "Son of God" is more related to His Davidic kingship (and thus His humanity), whereas His title "Son of Man" is actually the one that relates more to His divinity. While there is some truth in this argument (e.g. Daniel 7:13 applies the "Son of Man" title to Jesus' divinity [and also humanity?], while 2 Samuel 7:14 applies the "Son of God" title to Jesus' Davidic [human] kingship), it is overstated. The "Son of God" title, despite having reference to the Davidic Messiah, is still, very much, a divine title in Scripture (see, for example, Proverbs 30:4 and Isaiah 9:6).

father of Joseph. However, instead of God's Word saying that "Joseph became the father of Jesus," it merely says of Joseph that he was *"the husband of Mary, from whom was born Jesus, who is called Christ."* In other words, Joseph was not the biological father of Jesus.

The astonishing phrase here—the one which plays the first note of the crescendo chorus of the worship of the Son of God which is located in this verse—is the phrase *"from whom."* Again, Joseph is described *"the husband of Mary, **from whom** was born Jesus, who is called Christ."* This is an astonishing phrase, *"from whom,"* because it is feminine in Greek. The Greek text reads, *"…the husband of Mary,* **exs hēs** [the feminine form of **'from whom,'** where the **'whom'** must refer, here, to Mary, and not to Joseph] *was born Jesus, who is called Christ."*

Why did the Apostle Matthew write verse 16 this way? Why did he emphasize a break in the patriarchal line, such that Jesus comes not "from Joseph," but rather is related to Joseph only in that Joseph is *"the husband of Mary."* Why is it Mary, and not Joseph, *"from whom"* Jesus is born?

This is most astonishing, for it marks *a clean break in the biological line of the patriarchy.* Up until verse 16, the list of descendants from Abraham has been a *biological* list of patriarchy. Yet now, at verse 16, the father-son descent of biological patriarchy is broken. Jesus, who is called Christ, does, indeed, have a human mother. Mary is the mother *"from whom"* He was born. However, this sudden break in the biological line of the patriarchy is there to tell us that *Jesus has no human father.*

Here is where the crescendo chorus of the worship of the Son of God begins. Jesus was born of a human mother; He is fully human. He has a full human body, mind, will, etc. He does not merely "seem" to be human. Rather, He possesses full humanity through His human mother. As Jeremy Taylor, the great Anglican poet, envisions it:

The holy maid longed to be *a glad mother;* and she who carried a burden whose proper commensuration is the days of eternity, counted the tedious minutes, expecting the Sun of righteousness should break forth from His bed, where nine months He hid Himself as behind a fruitful cloud.[13]

Yet, most remarkably, Jesus had no human father. He was not born "from Joseph," but rather "from God." He is, therefore, fully God. He has a fully divine nature. This is not a half-human, half-God kind of Man. This is not the soul of God poured into the physical shell of a Man. This is not two Persons—one Person of a human nature and one Person of a divine nature—united in one historical Man. Rather, this is the one Person of the Son of God possessing—simultaneously, inseparably, and yet inconfusedly—two natures, one of man and one of God. The Son of God assumed a human nature. The Man Christ Jesus, born of Mary, is yet still fully divine.

This is an unfathomable and most praiseworthy mystery! The fact that Jesus was not born "from Joseph" marks the wonder of His divinity. His Father is from above. He is, truly, the Son of God. As Tyndale gloriously heralds in his *Notes or Glosses on Saint Matthew's Gospel,* "Christ bringeth God: where Christ is, there is God; and where Christ is not, there is not God."[14]

There is much mystery related to the "Son of God" in the Old Testament Scriptures. There are many enigmas

---

[13] Jeremy Taylor, *Jesus Christ — The Great Exemplar* (in *Jeremy Taylor: Selected Works;* ed. Thomas K. Carroll; New York: Paulist Press, 1990), 97, emphasis added.

[14] William Tyndale, *Expositions and Notes on Sundry Portions of the Holy Scriptures Together with the Practice of Prelates* (vol. 2 of *Works of William Tyndale;* ed. Henry Walter; Cambridge: The University Press, 1849; repr., Edinburgh: The Banner of Truth Trust, 2010), 227.

concerning the "Son of God" found in the Scriptures of
Israel:

The LORD says to my Lord, *"Sit at My right hand, until I*
make Your enemies Your footstool for Your feet."
(Psalm 110:1)

It is the elect of God, the ones who have ears to hear the
summons to repentance and faith in the Gospel, who are
intrigued by the mystery here and whose intrigue draws
their souls God-ward. In this affectionate draw of their souls
towards God, they ask, "Who is the Son of David? Since
David calls Him 'Lord,' is He David's Son or David's Lord?
Yet if He is David's 'Lord,' then how can He also be the *Son*
of David?"

The mystery of the Son of God continues in the
Scriptures of the Old Testament:

He answered, "Look, I see **four** *men loose, walking in the*
middle of the fire, and they are unharmed; and the aspect of the
fourth is like **[the] Son of [God]**.*"* (Daniel 3:25)

Those who are of the God-ward intrigue see the three
brave Hebrew men, Shadrach, Meshach, and Abed-Nego,
cast into the blazing furnace for refusing to worship the
image of King Nebuchadnezzar. They see the three men
walking about in the midst of the fire, miraculously
preserved from harm. Then they see one more Man, who is
"like the Son of God," walking with them in the midst of the
fire, and they ask, "Who is the fourth Man in the fire? Who is
this Son of God?"

The God-ward intrigue continues. They read in the book
of the Prophet Isaiah:

*Therefore the Lord Himself will give you a sign. Behold, **the virgin** will conceive, and **bear a Son**, and shall call his name **Immanuel**"* (Isaiah 7:14).

And upon reading this verse, they ask, "In what way is it possible that a *'virgin'* can conceive and bear *'a Son'*? Also, in what manner can the Son be called *'Immanuel,'* since Immanuel means *'God with us'*?"

We live in the times of the Gentiles.[15] It is the Gentiles who have seen what had not been reported to them, and who have come to understand what they had not heard.[16] The mysteries of the Old Testament Scriptures, which the Gentiles formerly did not possess, have now been made known to them, by God's saving power, through faith in the Son of God.

Yet if wild olive branches (the Gentiles) were grafted into the cultivated olive tree of God (the promises of Israel), how much more readily will the natural branches (the Jews), which were formerly cut off from the tree, be grafted into their own cultivated tree?[17] In the last days before Jesus' return to earth, then, there shall be many Jews who are intrigued, with a God-ward intrigue, by the mystery of the Son of God in their own Scriptures. For, they shall read:

*But you, Bethlehem Ephrathah, being small among the clans of Judah, out of you **One** will come out to me that is to be **Ruler in Israel**; whose goings [forth] are **from of old, from [everlasting]**.* (Micah 5:2)

And they shall ask themselves, "How can our Messiah, who shall be *'Ruler in Israel,'* have *'goings forth…from of old, from*

---

15 Romans 11:25.
16 Isaiah 52:15.
17 Romans 11:24.

everlasting,' and what does this tell us about the Son of God in the Hebrew Scriptures?"

The Gospel, alone, gives the answer to all of these questions:

> *...concerning [God's] Son...who was **declared to be the Son of God with power**, according to the Spirit of holiness, by the resurrection from the dead, **Jesus Christ our Lord**.* (Romans 1:3, 4)

There is only one path to God. Jesus is the *only* way, the *exclusive* truth, and the *non-substitutable* life, for He alone is the uncreated, eternal Son of God.[18] Apart from faith in Him—a faith which supernaturally and inevitably produces an exclusive allegiance to Him, including an exclusive allegiance to all of His glorious commandments[19]—there is no salvation, but only everlasting torment in Hell. For, the *only* mediator between a thrice-holy God and a wicked, rebellious humanity is the High Priest of the Gospel, who is the Son of God:

> *Having then **a great High Priest, who has passed through the heavens, Jesus, the Son of God**, let us hold tightly to our confession.* (Hebrews 4:14)

For wicked, rebellious sinners—and your own conscience, dear Reader, testifies against you, that you yourself have committed wicked acts against God's holy laws, and thus you have fallen vastly short of the glory of God—there is a sin that leads to death. Persistent, unrepentant rejection of the love of God as revealed in the blood of Jesus Christ, which was given to cover over your egregious crimes against God, is the sin that leads to death.

---

[18] John 14:6.
[19] John 14:21-24; 1 John 2:3-6.

To mock, whether by word or by silent indifference, the sacrifice of the Son of God, which was offered for the forgiveness of your sins, is an *unforgivable* sin. It has the power to cast both body and soul into Hell, where the worm does not die and the fire is never quenched.

There is, then, only one path to everlasting life. It is the path of repentance towards God and faith in His Son. It is the Son of God, alone, who has the authority and power to grant life to dead sinners, for He alone is the author of life:

> *We know that we are of God, and the whole world lies in the power of the evil one. We know that* **the Son of God has come, and has given us an understanding,** *that we know Him who is true, and we are in Him who is true, in* **His Son Jesus Christ. This is the true God, and eternal life.** (1 John 5:19–20)

The Gospel is that *the Son of Mary* is the Son of God. That is, though He is fully divine, He nevertheless has a real, human mother. In His incarnation (His en-flesh-ment), He is fully human. Thus Christ came in history; Christianity is essentially *historical*. We, as Christians, worship the Son of God who came *in real history* to save us from our sins. Without the *historical* truth of the virgin birth, salvation is impossible, for without the historicity of the virgin birth, Christ's humanity is a mere fiction. And if His humanity is a mere fiction, then He is unable to die *in real history* with *a real human nature*, in the place of *real human beings*.

However, the Gospel is also that the Son of Mary is *the Son of God*. He is not an exalted, angelic being. He is not simply a holy man, and the greatest of the Prophets. No, He is essentially God. In His incarnation, He still possesses *all* of the divine attributes. For, He is fully divine. The Son of God is not created, but uncreated. The Babe in Mary's womb is not finite, but infinite. Thus Chrysostom exhorts us, worshipfully, "Nay, for we are ignorant of many things…as, for instance, how the Infinite is carried, as unborn, by a woman."[20]

This means that there is no response to the Gospel of Jesus Christ that is half-way. There is no calling Jesus "Savior" without also calling Him "Lord." As Man, He dies in the stead of man. Yet as God, His blood is worthy enough to atone for the sins of all men. As Man, He lifts man out of his desperate condition of condemnation. Yet as God, He demands the full allegiance of man to Himself.[21]

Those who claim the title of "Christian" and yet do not walk according to the Law of Christ are not born again. They are charlatan Christians. For, one who is truly born of the Holy Spirit will be empowered by the Holy Spirit to walk in a manner that is worthy of the Gospel. It is written, and shall not be altered, that all true believers must demonstrate the evidence of their saving faith through *"holiness, without which no man shall see the Lord"* (Hebrews 12:14, KJV). This must be so, since the Son of God brings salvation only to those who accept both His divine pardon and His divine summons to bow down before His Lordship:

*Serve the LORD **with fear**, and rejoice **with trembling**.*
***[Kiss] the Son**, lest He be angry,*
And you perish on the way,
For His wrath will soon be kindled.
Blessed are all those who take refuge in Him. (Psalm 2:11-12)

---

[20] John Chrysostom, *Chrysostom: Homilies on the Gospel of Saint Matthew* 4.6 (*NPNF¹* 10:22).
[21] So says Richard Baxter in unequivocal terms: "I call it an accepting Him for Savior and Lord. For in both relations will He be received, or not at all. It is not only to acknowledge His sufferings, and accept of pardon and glory, but to acknowledge His sovereignty, and submit to His government, and way of saving; and I take all this to be contained in justifying faith" (Baxter, *The Saints' Everlasting Rest, Unabridged* [Geanies House, Fearn, Scotland, UK: Christian Focus Publications, 1998], 119.

The *Babe* of Christmas is both the Son of Mary and the Son of God. He is both human and divine. Therefore, the heart of Christmas is the worship of Jesus Christ. The Babe in the womb is the eternal Son of the Father.

Who, then, would dare to assault the baby in the womb, through abortion, at Christmas time? Is not every pregnancy (without any exceptions) an opportunity to honor the remembrance of the Lord Jesus in Mary's womb? Are not today's Christian babes of Christmas, and especially the precious, tiny martyrs of the Abortion Holocaust, with their fragile, little bodies and their gentle, loving kicks and thumps, all evangelists for Jesus Christ? Do they not proclaim, boldly, the historical truth of the Son of God residing in Mary's womb?

The King of kings was once in Mary's womb. The Lord of lords was once fed through an umbilical cord in His mother's womb. Yet He is in the womb no more. He is the Son of God, ascended to the right hand of His Father, and He shall come one great and dreadful Day to judge both the living and the dead. He will judge us, no doubt, with regard to our response to "the babes of Christmas," as they are found in Holy Scripture. He will also judge us with regard to our own action or inaction, and our own compassion or indifference towards today's babes of Christmas, whose lives are threatened by abortion and thus hang in the balance.

He was, in Bethlehem, the divine Babe of Christmas. He was born in human flesh as His Father's Son. He is, at present, the King of Heaven, the divine Son, who sits at the right hand of the Throne of God. He will be, upon the consummation of all things, the sole Ruler (the Davidic Son) over all of the kingdoms of the earth, for the Father shall glorify the Son with an everlasting inheritance in the saints, even as the Son shall glorify the Father in the presence of the saints with the utmost, everlasting glory. Amen.

CONCLUSION:
Found with Child of the Holy Spirit

"…she was found with Child of the Holy Spirit" (Matthew 1:18).[1]

She, the virgin, is found to be with child. God speaks life into her womb. The woman who has never known a man discovers that she possesses a Baby inside of her. From a newly-conceived Embryo all the way to a joyfully kicking Little One ready to be born, the Babe, Christ Jesus, is being knit together, shaped and formed, fearfully and wonderfully made in Mary's womb.

Mary is found to be with child, just as Sarah, the wife of Abraham was found to be with child. The words of Genesis 21:2, *"For Sarah conceived…"* are miraculous words. In her old age, Sarah was found to be with child. She who once had laughed at the promise of God now gave birth to her baby boy while others looked on, mocking her gray hair, and laughed at her. But Sarah named her baby *Isaac*, meaning, *"He laughs,"* and laughed her own, joyful laughter.

After Sarah, other miraculous conceptions took place in the history of Israel. When the Levite's wife conceived and bore a son in Exodus 2:2, the conception was not supernatural, but the saving of the baby's life out of the Nile River was, indeed, a miracle. The baby's name was Moses.

Then there was Monaoh's wife, the mother of Samson, who was barren and had no children. Yet she conceived and bore a son, only by the miraculous hand of God. So too was Hannah, the mother of Samuel, weeping the tears of barrenness until God heard her prayer:

---

[1] For poetic purposes, the present author has chosen to use the NKJV translation throughout this concluding section, unless otherwise noted.

*So it came to pass in the process of time that **Hannah
conceived and bore a son**, and called his name Samuel.* (1
Samuel 1:20)

Yet Mary's conception is unique. She alone can fulfill the
prophecy uttered by the great seer, Isaiah, the son of Amoz,
*"Behold, **the virgin shall conceive and bear a Son**, and shall
call His name Immanuel"* (Isaiah 7:14). She, and no other
woman, is ordained by God to be the very mother of God.
She is, indeed, a virgin, but she is found to be with Child.

The Christmas story begins not in a manger, but in a
womb. Mary first discovers the King of kings when she feels
the butterfly flutters of His first movements within her. Jesus
first meets His relative, John, when John is in Elizabeth's
womb and Jesus is in Mary's. Upon their introduction, little
John leaps in his mother's womb.

The glory of God first becomes human flesh in the
womb of a virgin. Think upon the Babe, Jesus, growing and
learning in the womb. One month He is learning to suck his
thumb. Another month He is performing somersaults in the
amniotic fluid. Still later in the pregnancy, He is listening to
His mother pray to God. She prays to the God of Heaven on
behalf of the Child within her, but perhaps unknowingly she
prays to the Child, Himself.

Mary is found to be with child *in her womb*, and so the
womb is the sanctuary of God. Jesus Christ sanctifies the
womb with His own holy presence. He consecrates Mary's
womb as the Temple of God. He glorifies the womb as His
first residence on earth.

God loves *all* babies in the womb, from conception
onwards, because the Son of God, Himself, was a Baby in the
womb. Therefore, all children, even those conceived in sin,
are gifts from the Most High. Children of all skin shades and
all health conditions are precious to Him. Babies with Down
syndrome are not mistakes. They are hand-crafted by the

Creator for very special purposes. Unwanted babies are wanted by God.

Moreover, God intends for life in the womb to be one of the greatest joys of human experience. He has created men to protect the purity of the womb, and women to cherish the gift of life in the womb. He has ordained the womb as one of the most sacred places of prayer and worship in the world. Many little ones worship God when they are in the womb. From the mouths of infants and babes He has ordained praise. Jesus called upon His Father in Heaven, even from the womb.

Again, "...*she was found with Child **of the Holy Spirit**"* *(Matthew 1:18)*. Here, in verse 18, *the Babe* in her womb is said to be *"of the Holy Spirit."* But then, in verse 20, *"**that which is conceived in her** is **of the Holy Spirit**."* A Babe, found to be in her womb, is of the Holy Spirit. And now, *"that which is **conceived** in her"* is from the Holy Spirit. *Who* is conceived in her? The Babe, Christ Jesus, is conceived in her. Yet *in what manner* is the Babe *conceived* in her?

The Babe is said to be *"conceived"* or, to use the old King James language,[2] *"begotten"* in her. However, this word, *"begotten,"* means that there must be a father of the Babe. For back in verse 2, *"Abraham **begat** Isaac; and Isaac **begat** Jacob; and Jacob **begat** Judas and his brethren"* (KJV). Yet Jesus has no earthly father. Joseph adopts Jesus, but Joseph does not *"beget"* Jesus.

The fact that Jesus has no earthly father is one reason why the Pharisees persecute Him. They chide Him by saying, *"We were not [**begotten**] of fornication"* (John 8:41), implying that *He* was begotten of a promiscuous woman and her lover. But Jesus, standing before Pontius Pilate, the Roman governor, says in His own defense, *"For this cause I*

---

[2] The KJV does not translate verse 20 this way, but the underlying Greek verb in verse 20 is the same verb *"to beget"* that is used throughout the genealogy in the first chapter of Matthew.

THE BABES OF CHRISTMAS

was [begotten], and for this cause I have come into the world, that I should bear witness to the truth. Everyone who is of the truth hears My voice" (John 18:37).

He is not begotten of Joseph. Rather, He is begotten of the Father in Heaven, by the source and agency of the Holy Spirit. This is just as the angel told the virgin Mary, *"**The Holy Spirit will come upon you**, and the power of the Highest will overshadow you; therefore, also, that Holy One **who is to be [begotten]** will be called the Son of God"* (Luke 1:35).

That Jesus is not begotten of an earthly father, but rather a Heavenly Father, is in fulfillment of the Scriptures. Psalm 2:7 prophesied long ago, *"I will declare the decree: The LORD has said to Me, **'You are My Son, today I have begotten You.'"*** With the birth of Jesus, not begotten of Joseph but of the Holy Spirit, this prophecy has come to full fruition.

What this means, however, is infinitely complex. To say that Jesus is not begotten of an earthly father, but rather that His begotten-ness is *"of the Holy Spirit,"* is to say that Jesus at once possesses both full humanity and full divinity. Mary is the *mother* of God, so He is, indeed, a true human being. However, Mary is the mother *of God,* so He is fully, and not just partially, divine. The Son of God, as the Son of Man, is begotten of the Holy Spirit.

What we are saying, then, is that whenever Mary feels the Babe kick in her womb, she is feeling both the little pulses of true humanity and the humble movements of true divinity. There are not two "Persons" mixed into one baby Boy. Rather, there is only one Person, Jesus Christ, possessing two distinct and distinguishable natures. The Babe has a human nature. The Babe also has a divine nature. And yet the Babe is only one Person, named Jesus, the Son of God.

It is here where the Christmas history humbles all human understanding. Since the Babe, Jesus, is begotten of the Holy Spirit, we can only marvel at the miracle of two natures, one of humanity and one of deity, united in a single Person. We cannot explain this. We can only believe it and let the power of the Gospel lift our thoughts God-ward.

Once again, *"...she was found with Child **of the Holy Spirit"** * (Matthew 1:18). The miraculous conception of Jesus—His presence in Mary's womb and the reality that He is not begotten of an earthly father—is only possible because it is *"of the Holy Spirit."* The agency of the miracle is *"of the Holy Spirit,"* for ever since the beginning of the world all creation of life has been dependent upon the work of the Holy Spirit. The first Adam was given life through the breath of the Holy Spirit. The second Adam, Jesus Christ, is now miraculously conceived *"of the Holy Spirit."*

That Jesus is conceived *"of the Holy Spirit"* is a message of hope to us, His offspring. We, too, are born from the Holy Spirit when we first believe. As the Prophet Ezekiel foretold, *"Then I will give them one heart, **and I will put a new Spirit within them"*** (11:19), so Jesus fulfills: *"And when He had said this, He breathed on them, and said to them, **'Receive the Holy Spirit'"*** (John 20:22).

As the offspring of Christ, we, too, are born, spiritually, through the agency of the Holy Spirit. Thus John 3:5, *"Most assuredly, I say to you, **unless one is born of water and the Spirit***, he cannot enter the Kingdom of God."* Or, Romans 8:9, *"But you are not in the flesh but in the Spirit, **if indeed the Spirit of God dwells in you. Now if anyone does not have the Spirit of Christ, he is not His.**"* Or, again, Titus 3:5 (and the last part of verse 7), *"...but according to His mercy He saved us, **through the washing of regeneration and renewing of the Holy Spirit**...according to the hope of eternal life."*

Christ's offspring are the fruit of His passion on the cross. We can be born again because He first died for us. As a Human Being, born of Mary, He bled on the cross with true, human blood. As the divine Son of the Father, conceived from the Holy Spirit, His death on the cross was the inestimable sacrifice of the blood of the Son of God. His suffering at Calvary appeased the Father's wrath against our sin. In His death, we die to sin. In His resurrection, we who believe in Him are born anew.

We are His offspring, if and only if the Holy Spirit resides in us. That He was miraculously conceived from the Holy Spirit points to the Good News that we are miraculously born again through the Holy Spirit. Therefore, we who are born from God, born *"of the Holy Spirit,"* are born into the family of God. We are adopted as children into the Father's household and by His Spirit we cry, *"Abba, Father"* (Romans 8:15). We are heirs of Heaven through the promised seal of the Holy Spirit within us. It is our rebirth, which comes *"of the Holy Spirit,"* which opens our hearts to receive the living water of the infinite love of God.

As such, as offspring of Christ, His Holy Spirit within us directs our hearts to worship Him. Just as the apostle John fell down to worship at the feet of the angel who had given him the Revelation, and, when he did, the angel rebuked him, saying, *"See that you do not do that!…**Worship God**,"* (Revelation 19:10), so too do we, the offspring of Christ, look away from the angels of Christmas towards the Christ of Christmas. By His Spirit within us, we worship Him. In His humanity, He is not ashamed to call us *"brethren"* (Hebrews 2:11). Yet in His deity, we call Him, *"Everlasting Father"* (Isaiah 9:6). Therefore, we fall down to worship at the feet of this Babe, the One named Jesus. His conception is *"of the Holy Spirit,"* and thus the glory contained within the tiny, delicate frame of this spotless baby Boy is an infinite glory. Amen.

APPENDIX:
Church History and Contraception:
What Historic Christianity Has to Say
Against Birth Control

"Whence [unmarried] women, reputed believers, began to _resort to drugs for producing sterility,_ and to gird themselves round, so to expel what was being conceived...Behold, into how great impiety that lawless one [the heretic Callistus] has proceeded, _by inculcating adultery and murder at the same time!_"

> **-Hippolytus (c. 170-236), _The Refutation of All Heresies_ 9.7 (_ANF_ 5.131), emphases added.**

"Why sow where the ground makes it its care to destroy the fruit? Where there are many _efforts at sterility_? Where there is _murder before the birth_? ...For I have no name to give it, since it does not take off the thing born, but _prevent[s] its being born._"

> **-John Chrysostom (c. 349-407), _Homilies on the Epistle to the Romans_ 24 (_NPNF¹_ 11.520), emphases added.**

"They who resort to these [i.e. wrong desires and contraception], although called by the name of spouses, are really not such; they retain no vestige of true matrimony, but pretend the honorable designation as a cloak for criminal conduct....Sometimes, indeed, this lustful cruelty, or, if you please, cruel lust, resorts to _such extravagant methods as to use poisonous drugs to secure barrenness [i.e. contraception]_; or else, if unsuccessful in this, to destroy the conceived seed by some means previous to birth [i.e. abortion]....

…Well, if both parties alike are so flagitious [grossly wicked], they are not husband and wife; and if such were their character from the beginning, they have not come together by wedlock but by debauchery. *But if the two are not alike in such sin, I boldly declare either that the woman is, so to say, the husband's harlot; or the man, the wife's adulterer.*"

-Augustine of Hippo (354-430), *On Marriage and Concupiscence* 1.17 (*NPNF¹* 5.270-71), emphases added.

"Although it is very easy to marry a wife, it is very difficult to support her along with the children and the household. Accordingly, no one notices this faith of Jacob. Indeed, *many hate fertility in a wife for the sole reason that the offspring must be supported and brought up*. For this is what they commonly say: 'Why should I marry a wife when I am a pauper and a beggar? I would rather bear the burden of poverty alone and not load myself with misery and want.' *But this blame is unjustly fastened on marriage and fruitfulness. Indeed, you are indicting your unbelief by distrusting God's goodness, and you are bringing greater misery upon yourself by disparaging God's blessing*. For if you had trust in God's grace and promises, you would undoubtedly be supported. But because you do not hope in the Lord, you will never prosper."

-Martin Luther (1483-1546), Commentary on Genesis 30:2, *Luther's Works* (St. Louis: Concordia Publishing House, 1958), 5:332, emphases added.

"*The voluntary spilling of semen outside of intercourse between man and woman is a monstrous thing*. Deliberately to withdraw from coitus in order that semen may fall on the ground is doubly monstrous. *For this is to extinguish the hope of the race and to kill before he is born the hoped-for offspring*. This impiety is especially condemned, now by the Spirit through Moses' mouth, that Onan, *as it were, by a violent abortion*, no less cruelly than filthily cast upon the ground the offspring of his brother, torn from the maternal womb. Besides, in this way he tried, as far as he was able, to wipe out a part of the human race. If any woman ejects a [preborn baby] from her womb by drugs, it is reckoned a crime incapable of expiation *and deservedly Onan incurred upon himself the same kind of punishment, infecting the earth by his semen, in order that Tamar might not conceive a future human being as an inhabitant of the earth.*"

> **-John Calvin (1509-1564),** *Commentary on Genesis 38:10* **[which is curiously omitted from most modern English editions of Calvin's Commentary on Genesis 38], emphases added.**

"Another duty of husbands and wives is cohabitation and (where age prohibiteth not) a sober and modest conjunction *for procreation.*"

> **-Richard Baxter (1615-1691),** *The Practical Works of the Rev. Richard Baxter: with a Life of the Author, and a Critical Examination of His Writings* **(Ed. Rev. William Orme; London: James Duncan, 1830), 7:119, emphasis added.**

"...conjugal duties [must be]...subservient unto the due ends of marriage [which include]...*the procreation of children.*"

> **-John Owen, (1616-1683),** *The Works of John Owen, D.D.* **(Ed. Rev. William H. Gould; Edinburgh: T & T Clark, 1862), 24:405, emphasis added.**

"[Marriage] results in virgins becoming mothers...the propagation of children is the 'normal' end of marriage...*we do not believe in what is termed 'birth control.'* "

> **-Arthur W. Pink (1886-1952),** *An Exposition of Hebrews,* **on Hebrews 13:4 (chapter 108), n.p. [cited: 25 March 2013]. Online: http://www.pbministries.org/books/pink/ Hebrews/hebrews_108.htm, emphasis added.**

THE BABES OF CHRISTMAS

ABOUT THE AUTHOR

When grace abounds to the chief of sinners, Christians learn to boast in the Cross of Jesus Christ. Awed by the grace of God and the majesty of the Cross, Timothy Fan serves, pastorally, to remind Christ's people that they are God's image bearers, His craftsmanship, created in Christ Jesus for good works, and are, therefore, very precious to Him.

Raised in a Southern Baptist church in Denver, Colorado, Timothy studied chemistry in college and completed his seminary training in biblical studies. He serves as the pastor of Genesis Family Church in Westminster, CO, and is the author of *Divine Heartbeat: Listening to God's Heartbeat for Preborn Children*, and *God's Ordinary Tinker: The Life and Doctrine of John Bunyan*. He and his beloved wife disciple their five children in Aurora, CO, where they pray for a "Malachi 4:6 revival" in the waning, contemporary Church.

Timothy's historic-Christian "mentors" include John Chrysostom, Balthasar Hubmaier, William Tyndale, John Knox, Richard Baxter, John Bunyan, and William Wilberforce. From Tyndale he has learned that "we be called unto a Kingdom that must be won with suffering only, as a sick man winneth health....Who ought not rather to choose and desire to be blessed with Christ in a little tribulation, than to be cursed perpetually with the world for a little pleasure?"

Soli Deo Gloria. Glory to God alone.

"For of Him, and through Him, and to Him, are all things. To Him be the glory forever! Amen." (Romans 11:36)

TO OBTAIN FREE MP3 AUDIO SERMONS BY PASTOR TIMOTHY FAN, PLEASE VISIT HIS MINISTRY WEBSITE AT:

www.godcentereduniverse.com

www.ingramcontent.com/pod-product-compliance
Lightning Source LLC
Chambersburg PA
CBHW031624040426
42452CB00007B/657